Practical marketing audits

Practical marketing audits

A guide to increased profitability

JOHN NAYLOR and ALAN WOOD

A HALSTED PRESS BOOK

JOHN WILEY & SONS
New York — Toronto

English language edition except USA and Canada published by
Associated Business Programmes Ltd
17 Buckingham Gate,
London SW1

Published in USA and Canada by
Halsted Press, a Division of John Wiley & Sons Inc
New York

First published 1978

Library of Congress Cataloging in Publication Data

Naylor, John
Practical marketing audits.

"A Halsted Press book."
1. Marketing audits. I. Wood, Alan, joint author.
II. Title.
HF5415.125.N39 1978 658.8 78-2948

ISBN 0-470-26327-X

Printed and bound in Great Britain

Contents

1 Objectives of the audit, its scope and the responsibilities involved

'Many shall run to and fro, and knowledge shall be increased'
Daniel xii, 4

Although we recognise that there might be a certain number of potential readers who see the title of this book and go away thinking that a marketing audit is something to do with accountants nosing into other people's affairs, we have decided to stick with the title simply because it most aptly describes the content of this book and also because we believe strongly that it is such an important discipline that the term will become commonplace within the next few years.

We have nothing new to offer on marketing theory or philosophy. Nor, incidentally, is there anything but the remotest connection between the marketing audit and these regular financial audits that we all know so well. What the book does, we hope, is show in a practical and easily understandable way how to examine and assess the use made of marketing resources—money, materials, people and information—with the objective of finding the means to improve profits. No original marketing concepts are involved, no intellectual exercises, nor do we employ any complex mathematical techniques. But the way of looking at a business is somewhat different and we are sure that we touch on a number of areas which are comparatively neglected in very many companies. Primarily therefore, our aim is to provide a nuts-and-bolts approach which is applicable to the vast majority of concerns, whatever the product manufactured, or service offered.

Whilst the two are only remotely connected, it is worth looking at the financial audit very briefly and contrasting its function and objectives with that of the marketing audit. First and foremost the financial audit is a legal necessity in most, if not all, industrial countries. It is designed to provide a guarantee to the shareholders, and tax authorities, that a company's finances are all in order, proper controls established, normal accounting conventions followed and that the statement of accounts represents a true and fair view of that company's current state of affairs. This may be an over-simplification but in essence this is its scope. One thing is certain: unless something very untoward shows up, the financial audit does not generally offer advice as to how the company should improve its profit performance in years to come. Looked at logically, it seems surprising that all the average shareholder really wants to know is that the company is generating what he considers to be a reasonable return on investment and that promises for the future sound good. There is no real measure of efficiency other than comparisons with the results of other similar concerns which will probably be operating at less than optimum efficiency.

The marketing audit on the other hand is a management tool and certainly not a legal necessity. Only indirectly through the end result, has it any connection with the shareholders of the company (and one might consider it a pity that the results are not communicated in certain instances). However, the wording of the definition of a marketing audit, not altogether surprisingly, bears a very strong resemblance to its financial counterpart.

The marketing audit is designed to discover whether the use made of the frequently considerable marketing resources a company employs is properly planned and organised, sensible controls are established, normal conventions followed and decisions made on the best available market and product data. It differs from the financial audit principally in that it includes a fair amount of judgmental analysis based on experience and rather imprecise data. It has the added advantage, however, that it leads naturally to recommendations for real profit improvement.

Later on in the book (Chapters 3 and 5) we shall discuss some ideas from the Boston Consulting Group and its offshoots in the USA. One basic concept which they have established concerns the experience curve as it relates to costs.

In simple terms this says that as a company's or industry's volume (experience) increases, unit costs (in constant dollars) associated with the product deminish in a predictable fashion. This includes all costs: manufacturing, marketing, sales, G & A, engineering, etc. The important point to note here is that these costs do not reduce automatically. Reductions depend on planned actions such as changes in technology, changes in methods of distribution, increased automation and so on. We believe that marketing costs can clearly be reduced in a similar manner. And probably the best way to set the ball rolling is to conduct a marketing audit.

How, then, do we set about it? Where do we begin? And what areas does it encompass? Our approach is straightforward. We consider every single factor, outside pure manufacturing, pure financial dealings and routine administration, that has an influence on our getting the right product to the right people, at the right price to give us the right profit contribution. It sounds an almighty task but in fact this is not really the case if our activities are planned and organised in the right way.

The best way of tackling any major project is to break the whole down into a number of manageable pieces and then to segment the segments. This is exactly the method to use in this case. We recommend seven basic divisions and then propose a simple step-by-step approach through each of these. Provided the steps are followed systematically, the end result must be a detailed appraisal of the whole.

The following, then, are the seven divisions that we recommend:

(i) A study of the market environment.
(ii) Basic financial analysis.

(iii) A marketing systems audit.
(iv) A total review of the product range, including packaging and product costs.
(v) A detailed pricing audit.
(vi) A really hard-nosed look at advertising, sales promotion and public relations.
(vii) A detailed analysis of distribution, together with the company sales force.

The sequence is the one usually followed in marketing studies: working from the general to the particular. Knowledge of the market itself is vital to a complete understanding of any product situation. In a company we worked on a few years ago, we learned to our cost that incomplete market knowledge can be disastrous. Everything else was perfect but we had incomplete market knowledge and came a cropper. Hence the number one position.

The second section will probably be a surprise for many marketing people, at least those whose interests do not progress beyond the sales force, advertising, sales promotion and public relations. Yet any definition of marketing, and there are many, inevitably ends up with a profit objective. That is why we are all in business. It follows, therefore, that as the ultimate objective of marketing is to make profits, it is absolutely necessary to understand the profit performance of one's products or product groups. Not only that, but one should be fully aware of the trends in the critical factors leading to profit performance—revenue and expenditures. Given this understanding from a marketing point of view it should be possible to establish key areas for improved profit performance.

Within the marketing systems audit we need to look at: information systems, marketing planning systems, marketing control systems and, where relevant, new product development systems. This is the hub of the business and when organised effectively should set the direction and pace for the whole organisation. As is too often the case, however, it is also an area which can too easily degenerate into a mass of paperwork and figure-pushing for the sake of figure-pushing. The most essential thing here is to determine what is important and concentrate on this, forgetting the rest.

Obviously we need to conduct a detailed product analysis. Packaging too. But what about product costs? Does this really come within the scope of marketing? In many organisations they are part of the jealously guarded preserve of the manufacturing manager. Certainly manufacturing should be held accountable for calculating the costs and operating to them once they are agreed, but this does not mean that Marketing should not have the right to question them in the first place and participate in cost reduction programmes. As we propose later on, Marketing should be held accountable for product line profit contribution within which product costs play a significant role.

In few companies does pricing really receive the attention it deserves. It is a difficult subject, unglamorous and salesmen the world over do their utmost to resist change in this area. Yet an increase in price is the quickest and most direct way of increasing pre-tax profit. And of course, handled badly, it can create enormous problems. Under this heading we also need to examine discounts and related non-price variables.

Who can say whether all the money spent on advertising, sales promotion and public relations is really necessary? How much of it is wasted? Luckily for the advertising agency business there is no accurate way of measuring this. And never likely to be. But there are ways of reducing wastage and at the same time improving advertising effectiveness. Because of the large sums of money involved it is really worth the effort of ensuring that all possible standards, controls and safeguards are in force and being properly used. Money saved on advertising drops straight down to the bottom line on the income statement.

Not so long ago we were involved in trying to pull round a company in the USA selling a range of rather simple packaging products to industry. Sales had been stagnating for several years and costs were rising steadily, so the profit situation was beginning to look decidedly unhealthy. The sales force consisted of twenty-six men, most of whom were selling direct to the end-user, although there were one or two trade accounts. Selling costs were much too high as a proportion to sales. It was also found that the eighty/twenty rule applied to the industrial customers. This, together with many more facts, was found in a very brief distribution and sales force audit. The decision was taken to switch from mainly direct selling to an emphasis on selling through distribution. The salesforce was reduced from twenty-six men to nine. The top twenty per cent of direct accounts would be retained by the nine salesmen, who would also be responsible for setting up distributors to whom we would hand over the balance of our direct accounts. The result was that we maintained the same level of sales at a greatly reduced cost. This example serves to highlight the need for a regular re-examination of the way goods are sold and distributed. Just because it has always been done in a particular manner is no reason to suppose that this is necessarily the best way.

Whatever the headings, a marketing audit, in common with any other type of audit, is largely concerned with people. Most of the information, work, or activities we are evaluating is obviously the result of people's work. In view of this it is certain that unless the audit is handled with the utmost tact and discretion, feelings can be hurt, resentment or fear built up and possibly the information that is obtained will be slanted to cast a favourable light on the person concerned. Before the final report is written it is always advisable to avoid criticism wherever possible but to give praise readily whenever it is due.

Where do we obtain all the information we require? One thing we should never do is to rely too much on any one person or one set of opinions—however senior the person or however good we think he might be. This is a classic error in any form of survey. By all means talk to the man at the top, be he the marketing director, marketing manager or departmental head when you narrow down to specific elements in the marketing mix. But every answer must be cross-checked up and down the line. Hear what the marketing manager says and see whether this tallies with the product manager's view. Ask the sales manager and then the salesmen.

Certain complementary tactics are also recommended. Field visits with the salesmen are absolutely essential. You will learn more about a company and its products from a few days spent in the field than you will spending twice as long in the office. Make every second count. Question the salesman about the products, competition, distribution, the company's advertising, how he spends his time, his communications with management how they control him. Use your eyes whilst you are out there too. See how well he is equipped. Watch how he plans, handles and records his calls. See what sort of relationship we have with the trade and end-users. Check on merchandising. What does he do with showcards, literature and other material of this type? Talk to distributors and end-users. Record their complaints—and praise. Really make your time pay.

A visit to the factory should be on your list too. Ask to look round the stores and walk round the production line. See how quality is controlled. Sense whether costs are being held on a firm rein. Discover the relationship between Marketing and Manufacturing. Ask how good Marketing's forecasts are—and be prepared for a shock.

A talk to the finance department can also prove beneficial. Traditionally, financial people tend to regard marketing and advertising people as an airy-fairy bunch of money-wasters, but much of what they can tell you will be very useful. They know the trends in expenditures—or should do. They know the people to watch when it comes to waste (sometimes their view is slightly biased!) If they do not have the information you require, particularly when it comes to financial analysis, ask them to help you. From experience we find that the people in Finance are only too ready to help but Marketing rarely asks.

The very last question to be resolved is who should actually conduct the audit. For a company dealing with subsidiary performance, the answer is relatively easy: a senior headquarters marketing man should tackle the job. Alternatively, a senior man from one division should be asked to audit another. In a single unit company an outsider should ideally be employed to handle the task. If not, the general manager himself might tackle the exercise. Never under any circumstances should anyone be asked to audit his own department. He would be auditing his own inefficiencies.

How long will it take? Provided the information we require is readily available, not very long. Allowing for field visits, no more than two weeks. Possibly less. But it will be time well spent. We guarantee it. And the resultant increase in profits should prove the point.

2 The marketing environment audit

'Having lost sight of our objective, we redoubled our efforts.'
Old Adage

One of the main aspects of marketing that continues to surprise us is the vast number of managers, and businesses in total, who seem to know so little about their markets and the effects of their varying marketing strategies. We were recently involved in management discussions on the size and share a company had in a fairly traditional and large market within the overall office supplies and equipment field. Most of the management concerned had quite a few years' experience within both the industry and the company. When the questions got round to market size, growth, share, the difference of opinion was tremendous. The market size varied, plus or minus one hundred per cent, the market was either growing or declining at ten to twenty per cent per annum and the company's share was anything from ten to thirty per cent. Further discussions revealed that what was being put forward were the opinions of the individual managers. Opinions, not based on facts, but based on what they thought was happening, their opinions of three years ago, conversations with the odd salesman, or some irrelevant article they read somewhere. The sad part about it all is that the majority of companies know very little about their markets, size, trends, shares, or attitudes and results of varying marketing strategies. There are notable exceptions (Procter and Gamble, Texas Instruments, Caterpillar etc.) but they are few and far between. The gap between the 'knows' and the 'don't knows' is huge and the ratio very much in favour of the 'don't knows'. If you think we are exaggerating, then just ask the middle to senior marketing management of your company what they think the market size, growth and share position is for your products.

Someone once classified marketing managers into the following categories:

— Those who make things happen.
— Those who think they make things happen.
— Those who watch things happen.
— Those who wonder what happened.
— Those who did not know anything had happened.

The first category do not, unfortunately predominate. The lack of knowledge about one's market and marketing situation is both frightening and unforgivable. It is like setting out to drive from Brussels to Frankfurt without knowing how the road system works, the principles of traffic lights, no map, and a car with blacked-out windows. 'Flying by the seat of your pants' is very much the order of the day in far too many companies.

Marketing in the seventies is still, and hopefully always will be, very much an art and not a science. Marketing is concerned with behaviour, with attitudes and with reactions. Notoriously, the most difficult predictions concern these very subjects. It is for this very reason that marketing decisions are the most difficult decisions a business has to make. By comparison, finance, manufacturing and administration are functions where decisions are more easily made and evaluated. Hopefully the art of good marketing will remain with us. That does not mean, however, that 'art' can be interpreted as 'gut feel' or 'seat of pants' type approaches. We must utilise whatever scientific help we can obtain to aid our understanding and decision making, but in the final analysis, it is our interpretation of the facts, information and trends that constitutes the art of marketing. Without this data base of knowledge, experience and facts, we relegate marketing to its lowest form.

Let us now look at what we mean by the 'marketing

environment'. In reality it is simply the world that exists and immediately affects the business we happen to be in. Too many text books on marketing seem to move on to some supernatural plane of jargon and expressions once they reach the chapter on 'understanding the market'. Macro or task environment seem to be included in every other sentence. It is no wonder marketing managers revert back to their 'gut feel'. What then in simple terms is really the scope of 'the marketing environment'? It is a knowledge, understanding and, where possible, a qualification of:

1. The status of the market and industry within which you exist.
2. The effect on the market and industry of the economy, technology changes, legal controls and restrictions, social or cultural changes.
3. The changing attitudes and effects of the above on your existing or potential customers, distribution channels, suppliers and competitors.
4. An evaluation of your company's position within the market and industry.

If you are to conduct a meaningful marketing audit of a business or product line, the four points listed above are the logical starting points. Through good analysis, understanding and qualification we get the overall scene prior to getting down to the grass roots of the business. Unfortunately, to get this overall scene to be meaningful, a marketing man has to assemble a large number of details which have to be monitored and updated on a regular basis. This we feel is the first point where things start to go astray.

Overall status of market and industry

People often assume that knowledge of one's market and monitoring of trends and changes is somehow or other proportional to resources allocated to gathering the information. Another opinion group is often heard saying that it is all right for such and such a company because they are in a well documented and analysed market where industry and government publish statistics with monotonous regularity. Whilst it is true that it may be easier and more accurate if you have to operate within a well documented industry, it does not mean that you can just forget it all if you do not happen to be in that enviable position. Knowledge and understanding do not necessarily cost money.

When approaching a marketing audit of a business or product group, whether it be a known business or not, we usually start from a basic checklist of 'what ideally should be known' about the market—and then refine the checklist down to a meaningful and practical list of questions to be answered. A practical example of this is shown on Table 2.1 and Table 2.2. By completing this refinement process we are tailormaking the audit to the specific business needs and capabilities.

When conducting the audit we find that an initial discussion, based on the questions in the refined checklist, enables you to:

Gain an adequate understanding of the overall position of the company in the market.
Obtain a view of the total market, industry and competition.
Establish whether or not the marketing management of the company have adequate knowledge and understanding of the total marketing situation.

Following these discussions a *short* summary can be written, highlighting the main conclusions. It is very wise to obtain management agreement to this document as this can save many arguments and wasted time and effort as you get deeper into the audit.

Competition analysis

The checklist in Table 2.2 gave us an overview of the results of competitive activity, but it lacked analysis and comment on the strategies that competition utilises in the marketplace. The

Table 2.1 Market audit — what should be known about each market

A The major areas of knowledge

1. *Conditions and characteristics of country*
   - Geographical coverage
   - Demographics
   - Political environment
   - Economic factors and trends
   - Historical attitudes
2. *Major characteristics of market*
   - Size (units—value)
   - Growth trends
   - Scope of products
   - Price level and trends
   - Factors influencing market
   - Overall status of industry
3. *Customers*
   - Who are priority target groups?
   - Who are large customers?
   - Who influences customers' buying decisions?
   - Reputation of company, management
   - Attitudes towards price
4. *Competition*
   - Major competitors
   - Size
   - Market standing, reputation
   - Market coverage
   - Market share
   - Marketing methods
   - Financial position
   - Distribution strengths
   - Production capacity
   - International link-ups and production facilities
   - Strong and weak points

B. The technical aspects of the market

1. *Organisation of distribution*
   - Trade associations
   - Governmental organisations
   - Wholesale and retail trade
   - Price and/or area cartels
   - Direct sales or intermediaries
   - Terms and conditions of sale
   - Normal trade practices
   - Official regulations
2. *Import regulations*
   - Free imports or system of licences
   - Quotas
   - Duties and influence of origin
   - Taxes
   - Conditions for duty- or tax-free importation

C. Characteristics of the product

- Special customers' requirements
- Packaging for transport and customs inspection
- Weights and measures
- Language
- Customer's quality and quantity inspection methods
- Official approval, inspection and verification requirements
- Labelling
- Consumer's quality inspections organisations
- Availability of materials
- Alternative material
- New technology
- Replacement products
- Substitute products

Table 2.2 Market audit checklist

Questions	*Answers*
1. Product description	1. Bookkeeping systems for small businesses
2. Market definition	2. Business record and bookkeeping systems
3. Geographical coverage of market	3. Total USA, with concentration on 40 major metropolitan markets
4. Economic factors influencing market	4. General economic situation and impact on expanding small business and new ones starting up
5. Economic situation and forecasts	5. Improved economic situation, reduced inflation, increased number of new businesses
6. Historical attitudes towards product category	6. Necessary evil of being in business, but law says I have to do it.
7. Market size in units	7. 1974 – 12 000 000 1975 – 11 000 000 1976 – 9 500 000 1977 – 11 000 000
8. Market size – value	8. 1974 – $120M 1975 – $115M 1976 – $105M 1977 – $127M
9. Historical and projected market growth/decline	9. Market has been declining in units. Somewhat offset by price increases.
10. Market share – units	10. 1974 – 25% 1975 – 32% 1976 – 32% 1977 – 34%
11. Market share – value	11. 1974 – 25% 1975 – 27% 1976 – 25% 1977 – 28%
12. Price levels and trends	12. Overall prices have been increasing at +/–5% per annum. Have not increased their prices with market.
13. Prime target groups	13. Small businesses (1–5 people) in major metropolitan markets
14. Existing customer quantification	14. Do not sell direct
15. Company reputation	15. Good, solid, slightly old fashioned, but reliable products offer good value for money
16. Customer purchase habits	16. Primarily at start up of business, end of financial year or at periods of growth
17. Major competitors	17. Business Books Inc. Globe Business Books Inc. Standard Books Inc.
18. Competitors' size	18. – BB Inc. $40M – GBB Inc. $1.8M – SB Inc. $100M (only $15M in competitive products)
19. Coverage	19. All national coverage
20. Competitive market share (units)	20. 1975 – BB 38% GBB 15% SB 15% 1976 – BB 36% GBB 17% SB 15%

	1977 – BB 34% GBB 17% SB 15%
21. Competitive strengths and weaknesses	21. Business Books Inc. Market leader – good distribution and good product range – high pricing—well thought of by distribution and customers Globe Business Books Inc. Standard Books Inc. Both are somewhat weak in both distribution coverage and in product offering. Tend to price-cut and use extra discount to maintain position at distribution
22. Distribution	22. Stationery and office supplies National coverage Most stock 2 – 3 brands Traditional product Little real promotional effort put behind product Poor displays
23. Distribution trends	23. No change
24. Product range	24. Wide range of books, forms, ledgers
25. Product costs	25. Projected to rise with increased cost of paper +/– 8% per annum.
26. Product changes	26. With changes to tax laws certain products will have to be updated

next step in the audit of the marketing environment is both to analyse and compare all major competitors' strategies against your own. Experience has shown us that either this type of analysis and comparison is not completed at all, or people write books on it. Obviously something in the middle is required, and as we are lovers of short, telegram style summaries, we often find that a simple checklist format can easily be developed as the most effective means of communicating these comparisons.

The competitive comparisons we should make include:

Market share positions. Based on units and sales.

Brand names.

Sales volumes. In total and split by product, market segment and distribution channel.

Unit volumes. In total and split by product, market segment and distribution channel.

Product range. Full comparison including features, packaging, performance, characteristics, etc.

New product launch. Details of new products in last twelve months including success/failure position.

Price comparison. Including discounts, special bids, etc.

Distribution coverage. Including percentage increase/decrease over previous year.

Sales force coverage. Including percentage increase/decrease over previous year.

Top ten accounts. Historical and current volume of each account.

Media expenditure.

Marketing strategy.

Promotion activity. Full details of all promotions.

In many cases the specific quantified information can be displayed in table and figure form to aid speedy understanding (see Table 2.3 and Figure 2.1).

Figure 2.1 Artist Oil Paint — percentage segment market share

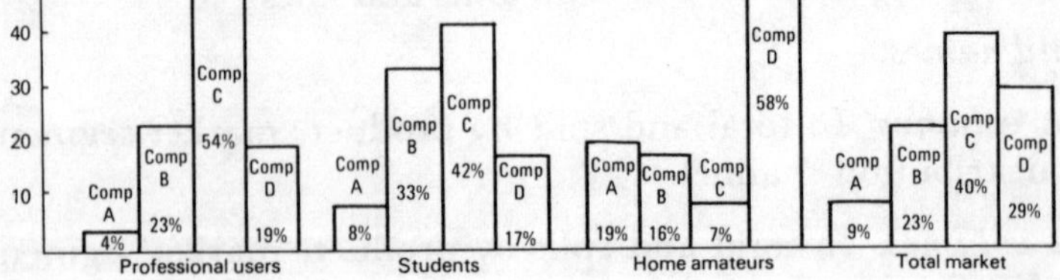

Displays such as these may be completed for all types of breakdown of competition—product, distribution, market

Table 2.3 Artist Oil Paint – Comparative market share

000's omitted

Market Segment	*Company Brand Units*	*%*	*Competitor B Units*	*%*	*Competitor C Units*	*%*	*Competitor D Units*	*%*	*Total Units*	*%*
Professional users	60	2	360	12	850	29	300	10	1570	53
Students	50	2	200	7	250	8	100	3	600	20
Home amateurs	150	5	120	4	50	2	450	16	770	27
Total	260	9	680	23	1150	39	850	29	2940	100

NB % is share of total market

segment, etc. At this stage we have kept much of the competitive analysis simple. The detail not covered here is covered in the specific chapters on products, distribution and so on.

At this stage of the audit we are looking for the overall position competition holds within the total market. This can be either very detailed, or summarised, with the fine detail in the specific functional parts of the audit.

Evaluation of the company's position within the total market

The data already collected give a detailed view of your position in the market plus an adequate analysis and comparison of competition. However this view tends to be one-dimensional and falls somewhat short of providing the auditor with the total perspective he needs. We have worked with many techniques over the years that give this added perspective but probably the best and simplest, is the technique of displaying your historical and current performance on growth/share and market growth/product growth charts. As well as readily communicating your position at a glance, they can also be used to display competition, thus adding the comparison dimension. Originally the technique was developed as part of the analysis technique for corporate portfolio evaluation, but we have found these displays equally effective when used for market and competitive positions.

The market growth/share display in Figure 2.2 illustrates the following:

Market growth. This is the compounded annual growth rate being projected for the market. Use as many years forward as is relevant to your business. Growth rate may be based on sales volume or units. If sales volume is used, then constant values of currency must be used.

Relative market share. This number is calculated by taking your market share and dividing it by the largest competitor's

Figure 2.2 Market growth/share display

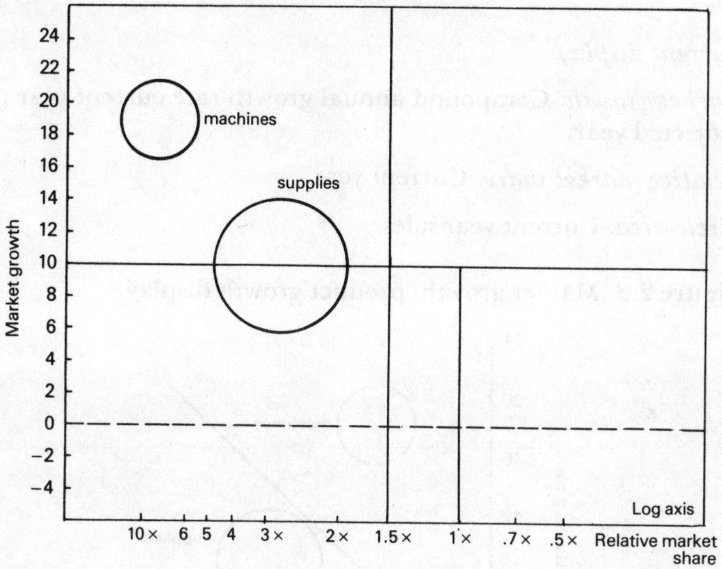

share. Therefore, if your relative market share is above 1× it means you are the market leader. Below 1× you are a follower.

Circle area. Proportional to your sales volume.

Axis. Market growth is linear; relative market share is log scale. (Log/linear graph paper is readily available from most drawing office supplies dealers.)

The display can also be used to record historical performance or the current situation:

Historical display:

Market growth. Compound annual growth rate base year to current year.

Relative market share. Base year.

Circle area. Base year sales, in local currency but converted for inflation to current values.

Current display:

Market growth. Compound annual growth rate current year to projected year.

Relative market share. Current year.

Circle area. Current year sales.

Figure 2.3 Market growth/product growth display

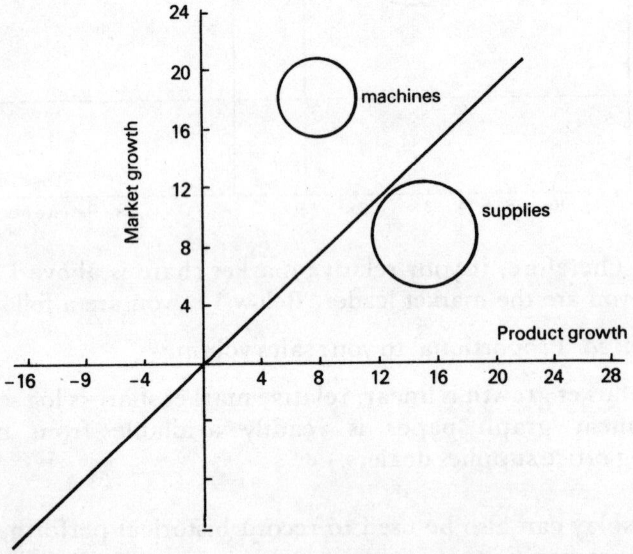

Figure 2.3 shows a market growth/product growth display and can be used to record historical performance or the current situation:

Historical display:

Market growth. Compound annual growth rate base year to current year.

Product growth. Your compound annual growth rate base year to current year.

Circle area. Base year sales converted for inflation to current values.

Current display:

Market growth. Current year's growth rate.

Product growth. Your current year's growth rates.

Circle area. Current year's sales.

Let us now take Table 2.4 as the basic marketing information available and develop the various displays. We can obviously see that the company is in a very strong competitive position with a dominant market share. But just how strong is it?

Historical growth/share display:

As the market is made up of two distinct product categories, we must look at them separately, using units as our yardstick.

Market growth — compound annual growth rates.
This is calculated by using a simple formula.

$$i = \sqrt[n]{\frac{y}{x}} - 1$$

where i = compound annual growth rate
n = number of years
y = volume of final year
x = beginning year volume.

NB It should be noted that the number of years is always one less than the total years' figures, because year 1 is the base year.

Machines.

$$i = \sqrt[3]{\frac{280}{190}} - 1$$

$$= \sqrt[3]{1.474} - 1$$

Table 2.4 Basic marketing information

000's omitted

Actual results	*Company A*	*Competitor B*	*Competitor C*	*Total*
Machine unit sales				
1974	140	20	30	190
1975	150	20	50	220
1976	170	15	45	230
1977	190	25	65	280
Supplies unit sales				
1974	1500	300	300	2100
1975	1600	400	400	2400
1976	1700	400	400	2500
1977	1800	300	900	3000
$ Sales-machine				
1974	$1400	200	290	$1890
1975	$1480	200	460	$2140
1976	$1650	150	420	$2220
1977	$1800	240	580	$2360
$ Sales-supplies				
1974	$1500	280	260	$2040
1975	$1600	350	340	$2290
1976	$1650	340	340	$2330
1977	$1750	240	800	$2790

Projections				
Machine unit sales				
1978	192	25	77	294
1979	195	30	84	309
1980	200	30	94	324
Supplies unit sales				
1978	1900	400	1100	3300
1979	2000	400	1230	3630
1980	2100	500	1393	3993

NB Inflation 1974 to 1977 was twenty-one per cent.

$$= 1.138 - 1$$

$$= .138 \text{ or } 13.8\%$$

Supplies.

$$i = \sqrt[3]{\frac{3000}{2100}} - 1$$

$$i = \sqrt[3]{1.428} - 1$$

$$i = 1.126 - 1 \text{ or } 12.6\%$$

Relative market share:

Machines.

In base year company A has a 74% share of the market.
Competitor C has a 16% share.
Company A's relative market share is $\frac{74}{16}$ or 4.62×

Supplies.

Company A	71% share
Competitor B and C	14% share each
Relative market share	5×

Current growth/share display:

Market growth.

Machines.

1977 is now the base year.
Over the next 3 years machines are projected to grow at 5% per annum, so in 1980, units will be 324.
Compound growth

$$i = \sqrt[3]{\frac{324}{280}} - 1$$

$$i = \sqrt[3]{1.157} - 1$$

$$i = 1.05 - 1 \text{ or } 5\%$$

Supplies.

Projected volume in 1979 will be 3993.

$$i = \sqrt[3]{\frac{3993}{3000}} - 1$$

$$i = \sqrt[3]{1.331} - 1$$

$$i = 1.099 - 1 \text{ or } 9.9\%$$

Relative market share.

In 1977 company A has market shares as follows:

Machines	68%
Supplies	60%

Competitor C has:

Machines	23%
Supplies	30%

Relative market share:

Machines $\frac{68}{23} = 2.9\times$

Supplies $\frac{60}{30} = 2\times$

Historical market growth/product growth displays:

Market growth — compound annual growth rate.

Machines	13.8%
Supplies	12.6%

(from previous calculations)

Product growth rates — the company's compound annual growth rate.

Machines.

$$i = \sqrt[3]{\frac{190}{140}} - 1$$

$$i = \sqrt[3]{1.357} - 1$$

$$i = 1.107 - 1$$

$$i = 10.7\%$$

Supplies.

$$i = \sqrt[3]{\frac{1800}{1500}} - 1$$

$$i = \sqrt[3]{1.20} - 1$$

Figure 2.4 Growth/share displays

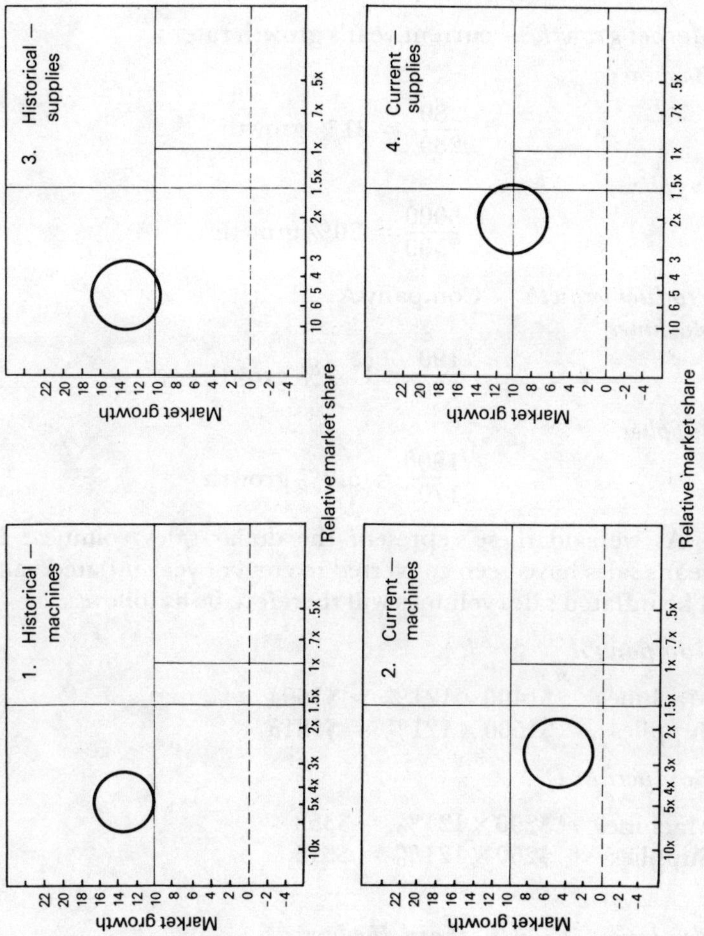

$$i = 1.062 - 1$$
$$i = 6.2\%$$

Current market growth/product growth:

Market growth — current year's growth rate.

Machines.

$$\frac{280}{230} = 21\% \text{ growth}$$

Supplies.

$$\frac{3000}{2500} = 20\% \text{ growth}$$

Product growth — Company A.

Machines.

$$\frac{190}{170} = 11.7\% \text{ growth}$$

Supplies.

$$\frac{1800}{1700} = 5.9\% \text{ growth}$$

As we said these represent the dollar sales volumes. Base year's sales have been converted to current year inflated values. The inflated sales volumes will therefore be as follows:

Company A

Machines $1400 × 121% = $1694
Supplies $1500 × 121% = $1815.

Competitor C

Machines $290 × 121% = $353
Supplies $260 × 121% = $315.

Analysis — growth/share displays:

The displays in Figure 2.4 readily show us a number of important factors about the market:

The machine market is not projected to grow at the same

rate as it has been. It has been moved from the high growth quadrant down to the low growth one.
At the same time the company's relative market share has slipped and we are no longer as dominant as we were.
At constant $ values, corrected for inflation, our volume shows some growth, but not much.
The supplies market is showing the same trend, but not to the same degree.
Our sales volume is static.
We are becoming less dominant in the market.

These factors must be taken into account when we look at the future, because whilst we are still the brand leader, the market for machines shows slow growth. We could spend efforts in the supplies market because there reasonable growth is still being projected.

Market/product growth displays:

The displays in Figure 2.5 emphasise our market position even more clearly:

In the machine market we historically have grown at a slower rate than the total market—and this is projected to continue, with the growth difference getting larger.
The same pattern is also seen in the supplies market.

So whilst the original figures indicated we were in a strong position, the displays show us just how much ground we have lost in the four years, and how this is projected to continue at an increasing rate.

Competitor's position—comparative displays

As a final input to our total market appreciation, we can include on the displays our major competitor (Figure 2.6) and then we can see just how much he has caught up with us over the years (Figure 2.7). We still lead the market, but it is clear we are fast losing our dominant hold on it.

Figure 2.5 Market/product growth displays

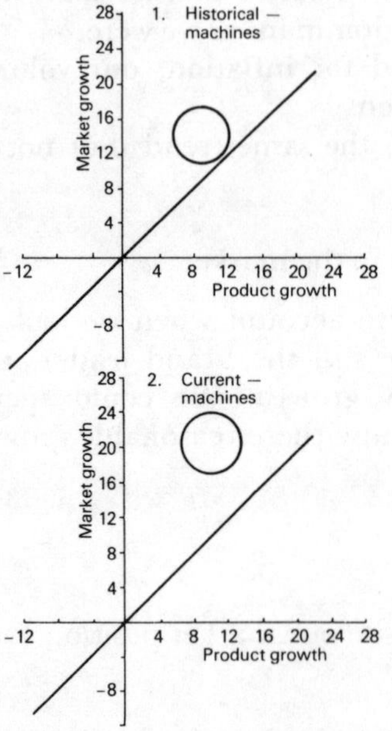

Conclusion

We hope this does not seem all too mathematical—that is not our intention. Our intention is to try to look objectively at the overall market environment within which a business has to exist. In most audits we find a tremendous number of qualitative statements are made about the market environment, but all too few quantitative ones. Our objective is to redress that situation.

Naturally, one still needs the qualitative statement, but we have concentrated on trying to analysise the total market, not just in a practical way, but also in a way which senior or corporate management will easily relate to. Finance and strategic planners do rule the boardroom. As marketeers our techniques must be adaptive, we must talk their language. Above all we must, if the opportunity exists, ensure we obtain the resources required and then efficiently use them to improve the overall profits of the company. The analysis work we have just completed should provide the input we require to understand fully the overall position of the company in the market place. From this point we can now move on to the detail functional parts of the marketing audit.

Key audit points

1. Have you collated all the relevant market data available?
2. Remember the environment audit is designed to understand the company's real position, not to evaluate its performance.
3. Make full use of industry and competitors' information. Annual general reports often contain valuable information.
4. Use practical checklists where possible. If management does not know critical information, find it out from other sources before you continue the audit.
5. Make full use of displays, charts, etc. to explain what you think the real competitive position is.
6. If some part of the market information just does not exist, then use a consensus of opinion to guess—but afterwards make sure you check it.

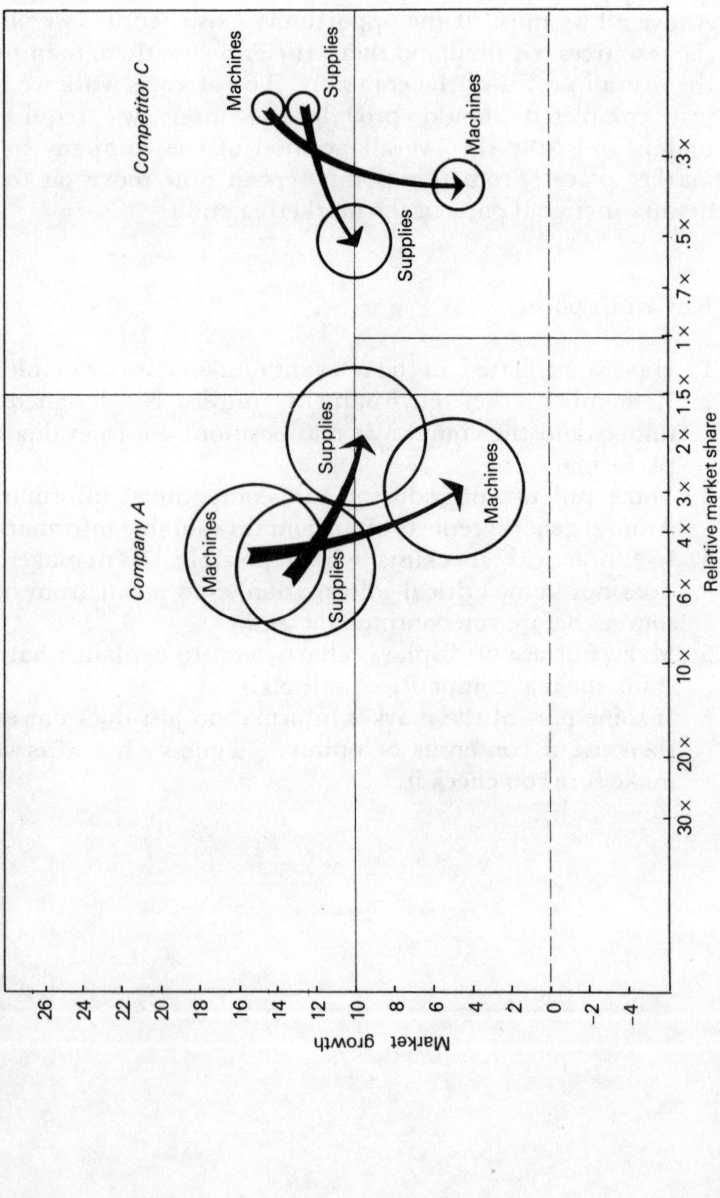

Figure 2.6 Growth/share display

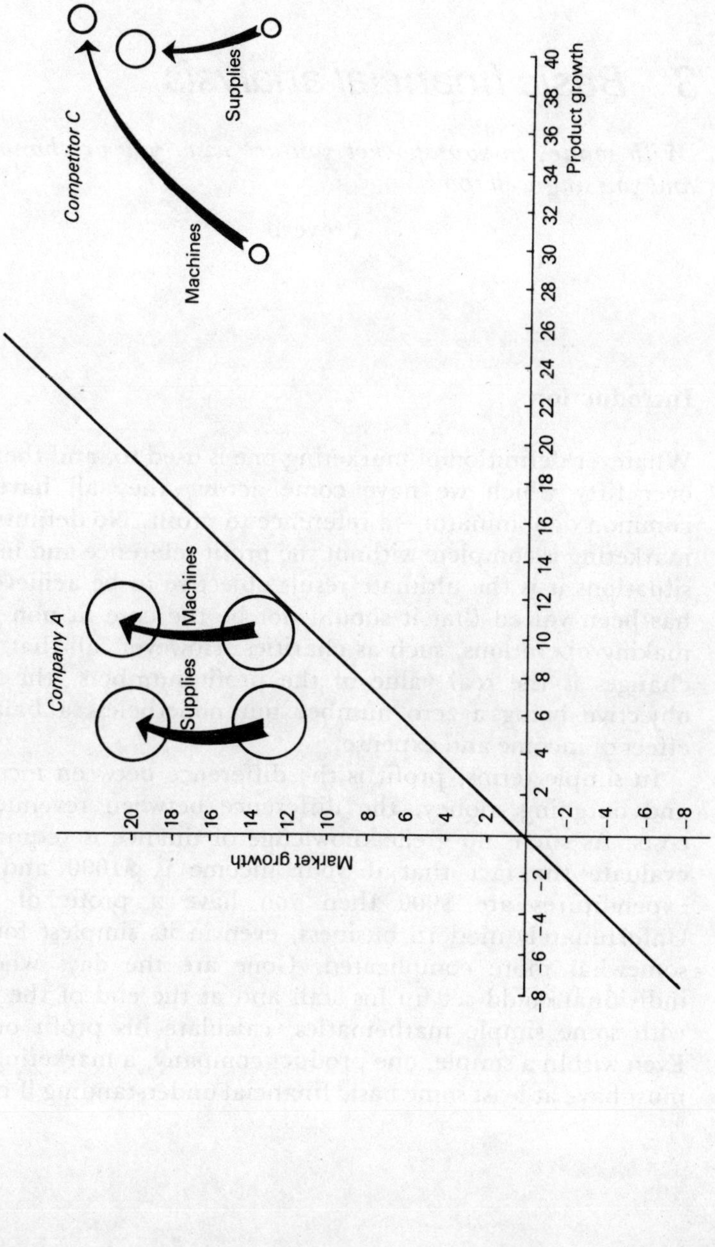

Figure 2.7 Market growth/product growth display

3 Basic financial analysis

'With money in your pocket you are wise, you are handsome and you sing well too.'

Proverb

Introduction

Whatever definition of marketing one is used to, and there are over fifty which we have come across, they all have one common denominator—a reference to profit. No definition of marketing is complete without the profit reference and in most situations it is the ultimate result objective to be achieved. It has been voiced that it should not be the case in non-profit making operations, such as charities. However, all that really changes is the real value of the profit numbers, the profit objective being a zero number but nonetheless a balanced effect of income and expense.

In simple terms, profit is the difference between incoming and outgoing money, the difference between revenue and costs. As such, no great knowledge of finance is required to evaluate the fact that if your income is $1000 and your expenditures are $900 then you have a profit of $100. Unfortunately modern business, even in its simplest form, is somewhat more complicated. Gone are the days when an individual could set up his stall and at the end of the week, with some simple mathematics, calculate his profit or loss. Even within a simple, one product company, a marketing man must have at least some basic financial understanding if he is to be truly effective.

To complete this part of the audit a basic understanding of the financial terms, criteria and performance is required. We do not believe that the marketing man should be a financial controller in disguise—he should, however, be able to hold his own in financial discussions as they relate to the performance of his product, company or division. We hold in poor esteem the marketing man who brags about his product's market share but does not know or understand the profits his products contribute to the total business.

Looking at marketing's role in modern business, we cannot help but notice a changing position which it is taking within the functional areas of the business. In the heady growth days of the fifties and sixties marketing was a functional god, like coloured shirts; who would be seen without an important, visible marketing department? The marketing department became the focal functional activity, with other functions supporting or reacting to it. Despite its frequent lack of line control and authority, it became the base decision maker. Suddenly those days of low cost labour, available and low cost materials came to an end. Middle East oil problems effectively put the coffin lid on that chapter of business history. The world saw the emergence of high cost labour, high cost materials and material shortages, which all contributed towards a slowdown in growth, and the high cost of cash became the dominant business discussion point.

As we entered the seventies the changing economics of the world were reflected in a changing position that the marketing function held within the business unit. It no longer held the key power position. Finance and strategic planning became the focal functional business activity. The need to manage the present and the future from a cash viewpoint became the dominant business activity. We saw the rise of a new breed of animal in business who analysed and evaluated strategies in terms of cash use and generation, and who saw cash cows and business dogs. Hand in hand the strategic planners and finance changed the power base within the corporation. The criteria became a progression from growth to maintenance to harvesting to termination, with marketing playing a role in each activity, but no longer as the base decision maker. To survive in this new jungle of cows and dogs the marketing man's financial acumen had to be greater than ever before. The financial data he is expected to provide the management goes far beyond the sales and margin figures. It seems, therefore, that the profitability analysis should be a focal point of a marketing audit, not just from a logic viewpoint but also from the point of satisfying the requirements of today's business management.

Objectives of the audit

1. To understand fully the profit performance of the individual products or product groupings and the total business.
2. To understand the historical trend of the critical factors which contribute towards the overall profit performance.
3. From the analysis and understanding to establish the key area for improved performance.

We think it also needs saying that the profitability analysis should be conducted from a marketing viewpoint: remember we are not financial auditors.

Basic financial reports

Under normal circumstances anyone conducting a marketing audit is also limited to the financial statements available; you cannot start generating all sorts of new financial statements just for the audit. We have therefore concentrated on the most commonly-found financial reports we have come across during our experience in both large and small companies/divisions in Europe and the USA. Because the world of finance seems to enjoy confusing us all, through its terminology and jargon, a simple glossary of terms, which we have found more than useful, is included at the end of this chapter. There exist within any business, numerous financial reports and statements, profit and loss statements, balance sheets, contribution statements, cash flow reports, receivables and so on. Circling a city prior to landing you get different views of the city as the aircraft descends and moves through the various points of the compass—so the different financial statements look at the product line/company/division from a different financial viewpoint.

Income statement

Sometimes called the profit and loss account. This is not the balance sheet but a statement showing sales, costs, expenses and profits for a given accountancy period. Normally this statement is a summary of the company's or division's activities and is not prepared by product. As such it gives us a very useful overview of performance, at a given moment, for the total business. Unfortunately, in isolation, it does not tell you much about the trends of the business. It is like taking your temperature: it is only meaningful from a medical viewpoint when you see the trends; so with the income statements to be meaningful we need to see the historical results as well as the situation today.

Whatever detail a company gives on its income statement, it always follows this sequence:

	Sales
–	cost of sales
=	gross profit
–	operating expenses
=	operating income
+	non-operating income
–	non-operating expenses
=	profit before taxes
–	taxes
=	after tax profit

For control purposes each summary line is normally exploded into a number of lines, as in Table 3.1. With this detail of historical sales, costs and expenditures we more clearly get a feel of the total picture of the business. We can see the trends of each line item on the statement. We see the relative movements of expenditures, costs, sales and the resulting effect on the final results. Depending on the particular practices of the company and/or country concerned, all income statements will basically follow the line items detailed on Table 3.1. However, there may well be changes company by company and it is important to obtain the make-up and content of each line item before you start the analysis. This often saves a lot of embarrassing situations later when the financial controller begins to pull apart the basics of your marketing audit.

Whilst the income statement gives the total picture of the status of the business it is nonetheless a summary and as such gives serious limitations to the marketing auditor. In most cases the business is made up of a number of products or product groupings and a financial analysis of these is essential if a meaningful audit is to be achieved.

Profit contribution statements

When a business is made up of more than one product or product grouping the performance of that business can be expressed in the following manner:

1. Let us assume there are three products, A, B and C that make up the company.
2. All costs and expenditures are either directly a result of having either products A, B or C—or they are a result of being in business i.e. non-directly related to product A, B and C.
3. In addition many expenditures can be expressed as either fixed or semi-variable on sales or totally variable on sales.
4. Financially, we can therefore report the performance of product A, B and C in terms of their sales and direct costs

Table 3.1 Income statement

000's omitted

	1974	*1975*	*1976*	*1977*
1. Sales	10 485	7315	8757	9287
2. Standard cost of sales	4017	3100	3961	4144
3. Standard margin	6468	4215	4796	5143
4. Total variances to standards	544	557	568	43
5. Inventory positions	104	73	87	93
6. Gross profit	5820	3585	4141	5007
7. General + administrative	637	659	693	732
8. Selling and marketing	3982	3088	3320	2942
9. Development	100	100	100	100
10. Total operating expense	4719	3847	4113	3774
11. Operating income	1101	(262)	28	1233
12. Interest and financial charges	330	300	333	307
13. Other (income) expenses	500	425	500	500
14. Total non-operating (income) expenses	830	725	833	807
15. Pretax income (loss)	271	(987)	(805)	426
16. Taxes	135	–	–	213
17. After tax income	136	(987)	(805)	213

Table 3.2 Product contribution statement

	Product A	*Product B*	*Product C*	*Total company*
1. Sales	2786	2800	3701	9287
2. Cost of sales (at standard)	1412	1512	1220	4144
3. Standard margin	1374	1288	2481	5143
4. Total variances to standard	10	10	23	43
5. Inventory provisions	28	28	37	93
6. Total cost of sales	1450	1550	1280	4280
7. Gross profit	1336	1250	2421	5007
Variable expenses				
8. Selling – comm.	28	28	37	93
9. – freight	80	84	114	278
10. – duties	–	–	93	93
11. Royalties	26	26	–	52
12. Total variable	134	138	244	516

Semi-variable expenses				
13. Field selling	280	200	400	880
14. Adv., S.P. and P.R.	250	216	370	836
15. Marketing	40	40	60	140
16. Market research	20	40	40	100
17. Other	—	50	50	100
18. Total semi-variable	590	546	920	2056
19. Product line contribution	612	566	1257	2435
Fixed expenses				
20. Marketing	60	60	80	200
21. Shipping	30	31	24	85
22. General and admin. alive	210	210	312	732
23. Sales office	55	55	75	185
24. Interest/financial charges	92	92	123	307
25. Other	150	150	200	500
26. Total fixed expenses	597	598	814	2009
27. Pre-tax income	15	(32)	443	426

and expenses and then detail the 'allocation' of non-direct expenses which the product carries.

The vehicle for detailing this is known as a profit and product contribution statement. Table 3.2 details a typical product contribution statement. Again, whatever details the company goes into, the statement basically follows this sequence:

Sales	
–	cost of sales
=	gross profit
–	variable expense
–	semi-variable expense
=	direct profit contribution

In this example we are seeing the product's contribution to the company's non-direct costs and expenditure. (In many companies these are sometimes referred to as general overhead).

By applying some form of allocation of this non-direct expense we can take the product contribution down to a pre-tax income.

Profit contribution
– fixed expenses
(marketing
general and administration
non-operating expenses)

= pre-tax income

The system of allocation obviously varies greatly, so before working with the product contribution concept you need fully to understand the allocation technique being used. The most common techniques we have found are based on allocating the non-direct expenses according to the sales volume of each product—the product's sales are expressed as a percentage of total sales. This percentage is then used to allocate non-direct expenses. It should be emphasised that, if you are to work with profit contribution statements you *fully* understand the allocation basis being used. Often, even within the direct expenses, there may be some form of allocation. This is particularly relevant to the semi-variable expense section.

The product contribution statement gives us a much clearer picture of both the performance of the total business and of each product or product grouping within the total business. If a contribution statement does not exist when you begin to audit, it is a very worthwhile investment to spend time with the financial controller and get him to construct one for you. Even if he uses forms of judgmental allocations to arrive at the expenditure by product, it can still give you a unique insight into the profitability performance of the company.

Whilst there are numerous other financial statements which can aid our insight into the business, we have found that concentrating on these two reports, the Income and Product Contribution Statements, we can gain, in most cases, a sufficient degree of knowledge and understanding. If, however, you find they do not give you the understanding you require, then you may have to dig deeper.

Analysis tools and techniques

Let us now look at the tools and techniques we can use to complete efficiently the analysis of the financial information contained in the statements.

Ratios

Financial ratios are one of the most important management tools. They can be calculated quickly and very often are more meaningful to a marketing manager than sheets and sheets of figures. They do, however, have limitations, but these should be recognised and not allowed to be used as an excuse not to use ratios. Financial ratios have often been compared to a thermometer and as such can be used to take the temperature of the business. They can be used to measure, comparatively, the financial status, effectiveness and profitability of the business.

In the final analysis, they are a tool which management should use and interpret as an aid to understanding the business. Too often we have found they become a means unto themselves. Too often we have come across managers who seem to have ratios mania—everything is expressed as a ratio, they make decisions based on ratios, they talk and think ratios, for all we know they probably dream ratios every night! As the rather simple out-of-town bank manager once said, 'Dollars, pounds, lire, marks, francs, can always be put into your account but never ratios.'

Obviously, there are a wide number of ratios that can be developed from the basic financial statements every company produces. The art is to select the right ratios better to understand a given situation. In most marketing audits we have found a limited number of ratios are important in giving that further insight into the company's performance:

Gross margin
Gross profit
General and administrative expense
Advertising and sales promotion
Field selling expense — to sales
Shipping and freight
Total operating expenses
Operating income
Pre-tax income

These operating ratios are normally expressed as a percentage, i.e.

$$\frac{\text{Gross margin}}{\text{Sales}} \times 100 = \% \text{ gross margin ratio}$$

If we now go back to the income statement in Table 3.1 and express it in terms of the key ratios, we see the picture in Table 3.3 gives faster, more easily identifiable trends than just looking at the figures in isolation.

Table 3.3 Income statement ratios

	1974	*1975*	*1976*	*1977*
Sales (in $s)	10 485	7315	8757	9287
Gross margin	61.7%	57.6%	54.8%	55.4%
Gross profit	55.5%	49.1%	47.3%	53.9%
General and administrative expenses	6.1%	9.0%	7.9%	7.9%
Sales and marketing	38%	42.2%	37.9%	31.7%
Development	0.9%	1.4%	1.1%	1.1%
Total operating expenses	45%	52.6%	47%	40.6%
Operating income	10.5%	(3.6%)	0.3%	13.3%
Non-operating expenses	7.9%	9.9%	9.5%	8.7%
Pre-tax income (loss)	2.6%	(13.5%)	(9.2%)	4.6%

Once again we see the inadequacy of the income statement in isolation; it shows for example a high selling and marketing ratio throughout the four year period but one has to guess as to why this is so. Applying ratios to the product contribution report will give us a better understanding of this (Table 3.4).

So far we have looked at ratios in terms of historical performance and results of the business. There are normally four situations where the use of ratios can be effective.

1. *Historical results.* They tell us the relative performance of today's result set against history. They show progress and trends but they cannot be used effectively to measure real performance. We very likely end up measuring today's inefficiencies against yesterday's inefficiencies.

2. *Budgets.* They detail the planned and agreed performance requirements. Measuring actuals against budgets shows precisely how we are performing against what we said we would do. One has to be careful, though, as much of the comparison depends on the accuracy of the budgets and the assumptions used.

Table 3.4 Product contribution ratios

	Product A	*Product B*	*Product C*	*Total company*
1. Standard margin	49%	46%	67%	55%
2. Gross profit	48%	45%	65%	54%
3. Selling – comm.	1%	1%	1%	1%
4. Freight – freight port	3%	3%	3%	3%
5. duties	—	—	3%	1%
6. Royalties	1%	1%	—	1%
7. Total variable	5%	5%	7%	6%
8. Field selling	10%	7%	11%	9%
9. Adv., S.P. and P.R.	9%	8%	10%	9%
10. Marketing	2%	1%	2%	2%
11. Market research	1%	1%	1%	1%
12. Other	—	2%	1%	1%
13. Total semi-variab.	22%	19%	25%	22%
14. Product line contribution	22%	20%	34%	26%
15. Marketing	2%	2%	2%	2%
16. Shipping	1%	1%	1%	1%
17. General and administrative	8%	8%	8%	8%
18. Sales office	2%	2%	2%	2%
19. Interest/financial charges	3%	3%	3%	4%
20. Other	5%	5%	6%	5%
21. Total fixed expenses	21%	21%	22%	22%
22. Pre-tax income	1%	(1%)	12%	5%

3. *Competitive data.* If one is in an industry where competitive information is readily available then measurement against competitive ratios can be a vital comparison. Unfortunately, in too many cases that we have come across the competitor may be an inefficient indicator. Accountancy variances result in comparison problems but more importantly it is often very difficult just to get the information.

4. *Industry data.* For most countries these are readily available, either through government controlled agencies or through business publications. They give useful information on the average ratios of groups of companies within the same industry. Ratios then can provide management with one important tool for control and evaluation.

From a marketing audit viewpoint ratios provide us with a fast, readily obtainable tool to begin the marketing audit process. They can be used to both evaluate the past and to predict the future. But beware! There is always some financial controller who, because you do not ask *all* the questions, lets you blunder on, draw your conclusions and then politely points out some change in accountancy definition and practice which turns out to be the real cause of the trend. Somehow they seem to delight in this situation; as a standard practice now, when we think we have asked all the right questions and received the answers we need, we then say to the demon controller, 'Is there anything else you think we should know or you feel we should be aware of before we start our analysis?' Often he will delight in informing us of some obvious point we have missed. If the answer is 'no' and at some later date he reveals some bombshell at least we have the pleasure of justifiably being able to kick him round his office!

We have found over the years that there are a small number of situations that regularly come up which inhibit the real usefulness of ratios. These particularly apply if you are working in a multi-national environment.

1. *Financial statements.* Be careful using past data to evaluate current performance. It is only accurate to the extent that

the background and environment may reasonably be considered relevant to future activity.

2. *Market conditions.* The differences in the markets for the periods being compared—price changes, inflation, material/labour cost increases, taxes and duty changes, etc.
3. *Currencies.* Changes in currency rates of exchange which may have a dramatic effect on costs and expenditures.
4. *External comparisons.* Whether it be comparisons with competitors or industry classifications, there are great differences in accountancy definitions and techniques used within companies.
5. *Multinational environments.* If you are auditing a subsidiary where the financial statements are reported in the corporate currency, say dollars, and the subsidary's products are partly or wholly purchased from outside the country, then use the local currency financial statements as your basis for developing ratios; otherwise you will find the ratio trends can be totally affected by changing currency rates.

But most of all do not develop ratio mania. It is just one tool for management which we have at our disposal, and beware of the manager, however senior he may be, who walks around the office muttering 'Percentage gross margin is off' or 'General and administrative expenses are up to nine per cent'. That is like saying, 'My football team scored ten goals'—if the opposition scored twelve it puts it all back in perspective.

Performance against budget

Perhaps one of the biggest failures we have noted as we became involved in a wide variety of businesses is the lack of performance measurement against agreed plans and budgets. Most everyone does it for the current year but rarely for history. Yet, as with most things, the key to performance analysis is precisely this measurement of what we actually did against what we said we were going to do. When starting any audit we now find that, having collected the relevant data, our first analysis exercise is to measure results against plan. It is amazing the information it gives, not just about the financial performance, but also regarding the type of management you are dealing with. We well recall a particular situation where the historical results all looked pretty good; the trends, in a static market, were upwards with small increases in sales volume being more than well reflected in increased profits. Everything looked fine until we look at historical performance against budget. Then we found it—there must have been so many safety factors in the budget that come earthquakes, fire, floods, they would still have made it. Consistently they met their sales budget but improved their margins, reduced their expenditure and were way over their profit targets. Once is understandable, but consistency gives rise to further investigation. A simple technique we have developed, shown in Table 3.5, is to re-layout the basic financial statements and summaries used under the following headings, per year:

— Actual results.
— Budgets.
— Variance.

In fact these headings can be used for just about any financial document, however sparse or detailed. If you are conducting the audit at the time of planning, add two additional headings:

— Plan.
— Plan variances agaist current year's actuals (or estimates).

You then have not only an evaluation of the past performance against budget, but also the future set against today's expected or actual result. The variance on each line, whether positive or negative, needs an explanation. This 'reason why' input, together with the basic financial analysis you have completed, should give you all the required information you need to complete the financial part of the marketing audit.

Table 3.5 Income statement

	1976			1977			000's omitted 1978	
	Actual	*Budget*	*FAV (UN-FAV)*	*Actual**	*Budget*	*FAV (UN-FAV)*	*Planned Budget*	*FAV*** *(UN-FAV)*
1. Sales	8757	8500	257	9287	9750	(463)	10500	1213
2. Standard cost of sales	3961	3655	(306)	4144	4290	146	4620	(476)
3. Standard gross margin	4796	4845	(49)	5143	5460	(317)	5880	737
4. Total variance to standard	568	350	(218)	43	100	63	100	(57)
5. Inventory provisions	87	85	(2)	93	98	5	105	(12)
6. Gross profit	4141	4410	(269)	5007	5262	(255)	5675	668
7. General and administrative	693	680	(13)	732	780	48	787	(55)
8. Selling and marketing	3320	3020	(300)	2942	3120	178	3150	(208)
9. Development	100	100	–	100	100	–	75	25
10. Total operating expense	4113	3800	(313)	3774	4000	226	4012	(238)
11. Operating income	28	610	(582)	1233	1262	(29)	1663	430
12. Interest and financial charges	333	270	(63)	307	300	(7)	280	27
13. Other (income) expense	500	450	(50)	500	500	–	420	80
14. Total non-operating expense	833	720	(113)	807	800	(7)	700	107
15. Pre-tax income (loss)	(805)	(110)	(695)	426	426	(36)	963	537

* Estimate or actual ** against 1977 actual

Value added

During the late 1960s and early 1970s we saw the emergence of new consulting groups and major academic studies which were totally based on current industrial experiences, the PIMS study being a good example.

Whilst much of their work was directed at corporate portfolio analysis, some of the techniques they used are useful and readily transferable to basic marketing audit work. The first of these techniques is 'value added' analysis. Basically it looks at the business or product line in terms of the value you add to the basic raw materials (or purchased components) which you processed into finished products. It is a technique used to compare your performance vis-à-vis competition, in the prime economic activities of the business or produce group. In simple terms it says:

— Let us assume competitors and ourselves all buy materials and purchased components at roughly the same price. (Unless there are huge volume differences or one company is vertically integrated this tends to be true.)
— Each company then adds value to these materials to get to a finished product. It then adds further value in order to market them to the ultimate customers.
— What are these values?
— How do they compare to each other?
— Why are they the size they are?
— How do they compare to competition?
— Are they a real cost of doing business and therefore a barrier or necessary cost to competition?

The technique is really very simple and easy to use, and with the help of an interested financial controller it can give you an added perspective on the business. Most of all, it can aid your understanding of the make-up of the economic activities of the business. This is particularly useful if the business is new to you and you have competitive financial information available.

We add value in the following functional areas of the business:

— Production.
— Selling and marketing.
— General and administrative.
— Research and development.
— Financial charges/other.

The value we add in each area can be expressed as a percentage of the total and will thus indicate the prime economic activity of the business.

The production value added is the only problematical area and you will need the help of the financial controller. The total cost of sales figure is made up of:

— Raw materials.
— Purchased components.
— Labour costs.
— Overhead.

The labour and overhead costs are the 'value we add' in production and therefore need isolating from the total cost of sales figure.

Let us assume from the income statement on page 48 that, of the $4144 cost of sales figure, forty per cent is a result of purchased components and sixty per cent is production, labour and manufacturing overhead. The manufacturing variances have also been broken out, with forty per cent being purchase price variances against standards and sixty per cent labour and overhead variance. The splits of the selling and marketing costs are self-explanatory, with the exception of the advertising and sales promotion cost which is broken into expenditure costs and departmental costs.

From the detailed figures in Table 3.6 we see that the most important activity of the business is marketing, closely followed by manufacturing. Within the details of the expenditure we can also see the relationship between the various marketing functional activities. As many of the selling and marketing activities are service activities to both the market and our customers we can determine their cost relationship and as we go through the total marketing mix we will be able to relate this cost to the effectiveness of the particular activity. It will also help us to answer the questions as to whether or not we can afford, or should spend, so much money on each activity.

Table 3.6 Value added costs of company activities

	Actual $ value added	*% value added*
Standard cost – labour	2486	
Non-material variances	26	
Inventory provisions	93	
Total production	$2605	36%
Total	$732	10%
Field selling	700	
Commissions/royalties	145	14%
Sales management	180	
Advertising and sales promotion	836	
Other	100	14%
Research	100	
Marketing management	280	5%
Advertising department	60	
Freight and duty	371	
Customer service	185	9%
Shipping and warehousing	85	
Total selling and marketing	$3042	42%
Total other	$ 807	11%
Total value added	$7186	100%

Cash use/generation

The final financial aspect of the audit we will look at is the cash use/generation performance. A number of years ago marketing people almost never considered this aspect of profitability—it was strictly for the accountants. With so many business decisions and strategies being orientated towards cash use/generation performance, we believe that this analysis should be part of every marketing man's analysis.

Probably the most difficult first step is to determine precisely how the company determines cash use, or generation. It does vary from company to company, so whilst we give a formula below, please check to see that this is the one the company being audited uses.

Cash generated

reported pre-tax income
\+ net interest expense (income)
\+ internal fees paid to corporation and included in profit and loss statement
\- company tax rate
\+ depreciation included in profit and loss statement
= Total cash generated

Cash used

increase (decrease) in working capital
\+ capital expenditures
= Cash used

The corporate charges, for example, management fees, internal royalties, etc. which are included as expenditure on the profit and loss statement, are added to the pre-tax income figures, because they are cash the business or product generates; but for internal accounting reasons they are shown as an expenditure item.

When looking at the cash use/generation of a business, or product group we can more adequately judge performance if we look at:

The net balance of cash use/generation.
The ratio of cash used to cash generation.
The ratio of net cash generated to net sales.
The cash use/generation ratio displayed against annual product line growth rate, at the same time indicating a graphic interpretation of the real value of cash used or generated.

The method used is to calculate the cash use/generation ratio by simply:

$$\frac{\text{Cash use}}{\text{Cash generated}}$$

A ratio above one indicates cash being used and a ratio below one indicates net cash generation. One axis of the display in Figure 3.1 features the cash use/generation ratio, the other axis being the annual growth rate (based on sales values) of the product group or business.

Figure 3.1 Cash use/generation display

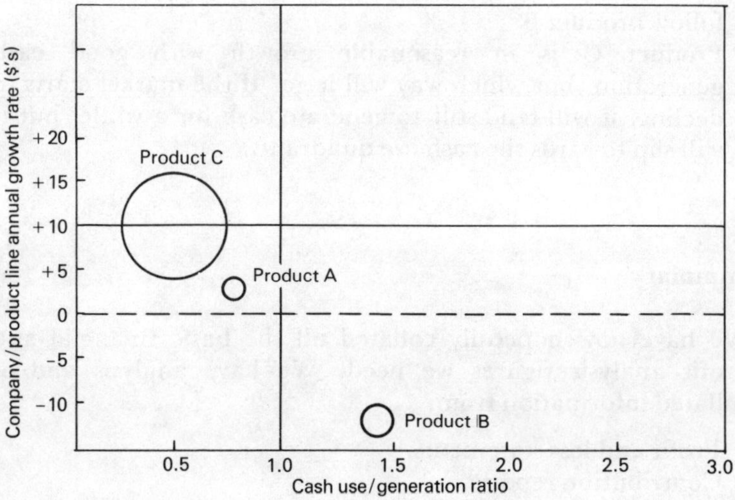

	Product A	*Product B*	*Product C*
Cash used	1500	350	350
Cash generated	200	250	750
Product line growth rate	+5%	−10%	+10%
Cash use/generation ratio	0.75	1.40	0.46
Net cash generation (use)	50	(100)	400
% to sales	0.01%	(0.03)	10%

NB. The circles are in proportion to net cash generated or used.

This cash use/generation display technique (more commonly associated with portfolio analysis work) is extremely effective for getting the various product lines in perspective. If one is fortunate enough to be able to get competitive or industry information, then you can measure your performance against their performance. If one is analysing a business as part of the planning process, the plan figures can be shown against current year's actual performance.

In studying the display we can see that:

Product B is using cash and is in a declining market.

Product A, with slow growth, is generating on marginal cash. It is unlikely it is going to grow so will eventually follow product B.

Product C is in reasonable growth with good cash generation, but which way will it go? If the market starts to decline, it will tend still to generate cash for a while, but it will slip towards the cash use quadrant.

Summary

We have now hopefully collated all the basic financial and profit analysis figures we need. We have analysis and/or collated information from:

Profit and loss statements.
Contribution reports.
Ratio analysis.
Value added analysis.
Cash use/generation.

We have also displayed this information against some qualified marketing information:

Product growth rates.
Market growth rates.
Market share position.
Competitive size.

We have, however, tended to concentrate on the explanation of the techniques and omitted the quantitative judgements of the information which is available. Let us now add this final dimension of the audit by looking at a specific case study.

Case study — basic financial analysis

Company background

A USA company in the art materials market. The company is old and well-established, but has shown little growth over the last three years. The management have all grown up within the industry and whatever company they have been with has followed the industry growth pattern of approximately ten per cent per annum. The overall market is still growing at ten per cent per annum (unit sales of paint). Generally speaking, the management remain optimistic, thinking everything will turn out for the better, and therefore implementing no real strategies to alter their current business situation.

The financial statements available are detailed in Table 3.7. Following discussions with the controller, a contribution report (Table 3.8) was developed for the two main products of the company—tubes of paint and brushes. The other marketing information available is detailed in Table 3.9.

Additional information

Manufacturing—brushes are purchased from Japan—finished and packaged. Out of total standard cost for brushes, the landed cost represents eighty per cent.

Paint is manufactured in-house with a purchase material value of thirty per cent of standard cost.

The cash position of the company was as follows:

	1974	1975
Cash generated	800	300
Cash used	400	200

Table 3.7 Artist Oil Company profit and loss statement

	1973	*1974*	*1975*
			(000's omitted)
1. Sales	5243	5524	5221
2. Standard cost of sales	3418	3741	3484
3. Standard gross margin	1825	1783	1737
4. Variances	—	60	—
5. Gross profit	1825	1723	1737
6. General and administr.	440	468	481
7. Selling and marketing	1100	1232	1304
8. Total operating expenses	1540	1700	1785
9. Operating income	285	23	(48)
10. Non-operating expenses	20	30	50
11. Pre-tax income	265	(7)	(98)

Table 3.9 Comparative sales and unit growth

000's omitted

1975	*Artist Oil Company*	*Competitor A*	*Competitor B*
Sales—brushes	1471	787	1900
—paint	3750	4700	4800
Units—brushes	3000	1500	4000
—paint	2500	3500	3800
Unit growth over previous year			
—brushes	—	100	300
—paint	(500)	250	600

Analysis

The profit and loss statement summarises the declining fortunes of the company. The sales trend is fairly static but the gross profit percentage has declined from thirty-five per cent in 1973 to thirty-three per cent in 1975. Because of the nature of the industry this decline is considered normal. However, from the profit and loss statement we can see that, despite the sales

Table 3.8 Artist Oil Company contribution report

	1974			1975		
	Paint	*Brushes*	*Total*	*Paint*	*Brushes*	*Total*
1. Sales	4000	1524	5524	3750	1471	5221
2. Total cost of sales	2900	901	3801	2775	709	3484
3. Gross profit	1100	623	1723	975	762	1737
Variable expenses						
4. Sales commission	200	70	270	190	70	260
5. Freight	200	50	250	200	60	260
6. Total	400	120	520	390	130	520
Semi-variable						
7. Field selling	150	150	300	160	160	320
8. Advertising	100	50	150	100	50	150
9. Marketing	50	20	70	50	27	77
10. Total	300	220	520	310	237	547
11. Contribution	400	283	683	275	395	670
General fixed overhead						
12. Marketing (incl. shipping)			102			130
13. Sales office			90			107
14. G & A			468			481
15. Financial			30			50
16. Total fixed			690			768
17. PTI			(7)			(98)

in 1973 and 1975 being almost identical, the swing in pre-tax profits is \$363 000.

We can see that the contributing factors are as follows:

Lost gross profit	(88)	due to margin loss of 2%
Additional general and administrative expenses	(41)	a 10% increase over two years within the bounds of normal inflation.

Additional selling-marketing	(204)	18% increase which seems high
Financial charges	(30)	in view of two years performance it is within acceptable limits
Total	(363)	

At this stage all we can say is that the decline is a result of:

a) Static sales turnover.
b) Lost gross margin.
c) Somewhat excessive increase in selling and marketing expense.
d) The company bearing the full impact of inflation.

We must now look a little deeper into the problem by analysing the contribution statements we have generated.

First, let us look at the gross profit situation to see if the contribution statements offer us more information than the profit and loss statement.

	Gross profit	
	1974	1975
Brushes	40.8%	51.8%
Paint	27.5%	26%
Total	31%	33%

It seems that whilst we do not have a contribution statement for 1973 (the controller not being able to split the costs) we can obtain some indication of why we have a margin problem. Paint, which the company manufactures, has a declining unit and $ sales value, whilst brushes reflect static unit and sales volume, but increase margins. We subsequently found this was due to changing suppliers. Taking some of the marketing information we can summarise the situation as follows:

In 1975 the company's price position was:

Brushes $\frac{\text{Sales volume}}{\text{Unit volume}} = \frac{1\,471\,000}{3\,000\,000} = \$0.49$

Paint tubes $\frac{\text{Sales volume}}{\text{Unit volume}} = \frac{3\,750\,000}{2\,500\,000} = \$1.50$

We can also see that the 1974 volume for brushes was as 1975, but paint was 500 000 units down.

The 1974 prices were therefore:

Brushes $\frac{1\,524\,000}{3\,000\,000} = \$0.51$

Paint $\frac{4\,000\,000}{3\,000\,000} = \$1.34$

The decline in brush pricing could be due to product mix or a marginal price decrease.

The paint situation is most disturbing. We see a fairly big price increase, too big for product mix, so it must be a real price increase in the market place—also confirmed by lost unit sales. The answer must be in product costing, and that must be where we look for the problem and the solution.

From the information provided we can also see the comparative price position, in 1975, of competition.

	Brushes	*Paint*
Artist oil company	0.49	1.50
Competitor A	0.52	1.34
Competitor B	0.47	1.26

This tends to confirm that the problem is in the manufacturing costings. We have the highest price and lowest volume, so little chance of implementing price increases to solve our margin problem.

Let us now look at the cost structure of the company. Let us also assume at this stage that the allocations of expenditures to the product reflects closely the true situation.

The first obvious problem is the low amount of really variable costs in the business. Fluctuating sales volumes are therefore felt immediately—increased profits if volumes are up and losses if volume goes down. This can be easily demonstrated by a simple breakeven chart for the total company (Figure 3.2).

Figure 3.2 Break even chart

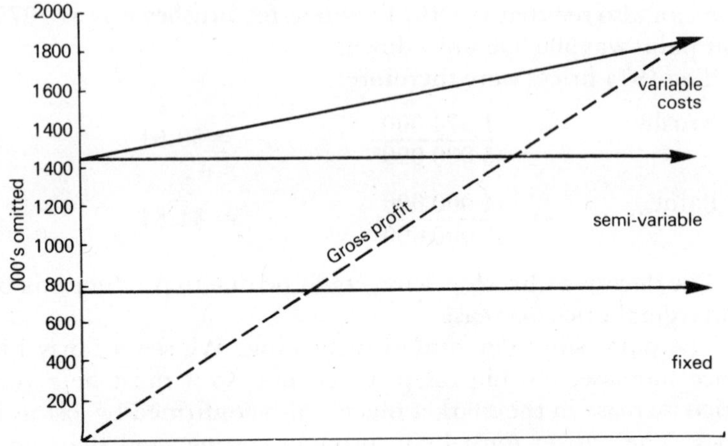

With a minimum margin requirement of $1958 to break even, this means at current gross profit ratios sales of $5934.

The company therefore seems in a very vulnerable position. As semi-variable costs are normally costs which take time to reduce, a small change in volume can put them dramatically in the red.

Before drawing any further conclusion we should look at some key ratios to see if they indicate any possible solutions:

From the 1975 Profit and Loss Statement:

Selling and marketing is 25 per cent of sales, up from the 1974 figure of 22 per cent.

General and administrative at 9.2 per cent is up from 8.5 per cent in 1974, but as it is a fixed expense and, in real value, only showing an increase of 2.7 per cent, it seems a reasonable figure.

We must therefore look at the sales and marketing budgets, but firstly let us look at the value added situation to see if we can discover anything there. From the previous information provided we can calculate the manufacturing value added:

Brushes	Total cost of sales	=	709
	Purchased materials at 80% of COS	=	567
	Value added		142
Paint	Total cost of sales	=	2775
	Purchased materials at 30% of COS	=	833
	Value added		1542

Value added — Artists Oil Company

000's omitted

Total manufacturing value added		1684		48%
General and administrative		481		14%
Field selling/commissions		580	16%	
Advertising		150	4%	
Marketing (less shipping)		147	4%	
Shipping	60			
Freight	260	427	12%	
Sales office	107			
Total marketing		1304		37%
Other		50		1%
Total value added		3519		100%

The most important economic activity of the company is clearly production. We know that our prices are the highest, our margin is decreasing, so unless there are some real economies of scale within manufacturing, we have a basic problem of production cost. Solutions could include:

Outside purchase of paint products.
Increased efficiencies.
Lower manufacturing overhead.
Lower packaging costs.

The other points we can pick up from the value added table are that:

Marketing and advertising seem reasonable expenditure levels.
Sales and logistics, at 28 per cent of value added, are 75 per cent of total marketing value added.

It is these two areas, sales and logistics, that now need further analysis. The general level of sales cost is obviously high at eleven per cent of sales. It would be interesting to find out what the industry norms are. Internally, further analysis work must be done to establish:

Territory profitability.
Commission rates.
Salesmen's costs.

Similarly the logistics require explanation, at eight per cent of sales—far too high. One should look at:

Terms and conditions of sales.
Freight method being used.
Minimum order size.
More use of wholesalers.

Finally we will look at the cash situation of the company—with two years in the red this could soon become the most critical problem the company faces.

For two years we can see the cash use/generation ratio is as follows:

	1974	1975
$\frac{\text{Cash use}}{\text{Cash generated}}$	$\frac{400}{800} = .5$	$\frac{200}{300} = .66$
Net cash generated	\$400	\$100
Growth rates	5%	−5%

If we need further evidence of the company's vulnerability—Figure 3.3 provides it. The company is fast slipping towards a 'dog' business—using cash and negative growth.

This financial analysis has indicated precisely where the problems are, and given us all the directions we need so that we know where to concentrate our audit—and we did not need to be an accounting genius to do it.

Figure 3.3 Cash use/generation display

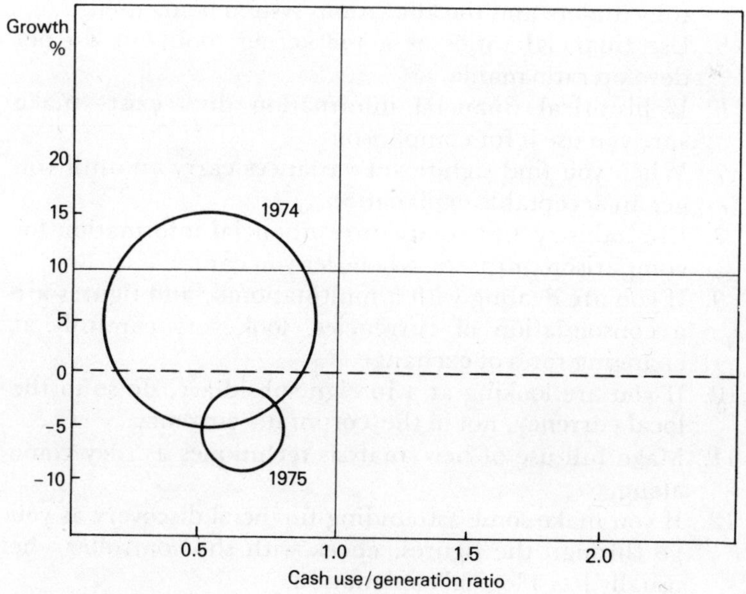

Key audit points

1. Remember Murphy's Third Law:

   'In any collection of performance and accounting data, the figures that are obviously correct and beyond all need of checking contain the errors.'

Corollary 1 – Those you ask for help will not see the error.

Corollary 2 – Any nagging intruder who stops by with unsought advice will spot it immediately.

2. Before you get into financial statements, make sure you fully understand both the accounting system being used, and the expenditures included in each line item.
3. Always ask what other financial information is available – it is amazing how much the accountants keep to themselves.
4. When dealing with contribution reports make sure you fully understand the allocations system being used.
5. Use financial ratios as a marketing tool, but do not develop ratio mania.
6. If historical financial information does exist – make sure you use it for comparisons.
7. When you find significant variances carry on until you get an acceptable explanation.
8. Use industry and competitive financial information for comparison purposes, whenever you can.
9. If you are dealing with a multinational, and figures are a consolidation of currencies, look very carefully at changing rates of exchange.
10. If you are looking at a foreign subsidiary, do so in the local currency, not in the 'corporate' currency.
11. Make full use of new analysis techniques as they come along.
12. If you make some astounding financial discovery as you go through the figures, check with the controller – he usually has a logical explanation.
13. Use the controller's department as much as you can – they can be your biggest asset.
14. If you do not understand – ASK.

Appendix to Chapter 3

A simple glossary of the language of accounting reports*

Account. Page in the ledger recording the common aspect of different transactions. Real, personal, nominal accounts.

Accountancy. Accounting.

Accounting. Art of preparing accounting reports from bookkeeping records. Based on accounting concepts or principles: true and fair, money, cost, conservatism, consistency, comparability, entity, going concern, recognition of profit accruals, etc.

Accounting concepts. Accounting principles underlying concepts which enable bookkeeping records of transactions to be converted into accounting reports.

Accounting language. The accounting meaning rather than the ordinary meaning of words.

Account payable. Creditor. Money owed by a business. Current liability.

Accounting period. Period of time from one balance sheet to the next. Period of the income statement. Usually one year.

Accounting principles. Accounting concepts.

Account receivable. Debtor. Money owed to the business.

* Reproduced with the kind permission of Professor R.G.A. Boland and Hodder and Stoughton Limited from *Accounting Step by Step Book 1: Accountancy Reports,* 2nd edition, 1970.

Accounting reports. Balance sheet and income statement (profit and loss account).

Accumulated depreciation. Current asset. Extent to which the fixed asset cost has been allocated to depreciation expense, since the asset was originally acquired. Reserve for depreciation. Provision for depreciation.

Accumulated profit. Retained earnings. Balance of profit retained in the business. Increase in owners' equity due to profit earned but not paid out in dividends. Profit and loss account balance carried forward. *Not* the profit for one year only.

Accrual. Liability. Creditor. Payable. Current liability. Accounting concept. Income and expense must be included whether for cash or credit.

Administrative expense. Cost of directing and controlling a business. Includes: directors' fees, office salaries, office rent, lighting, heating, legal fees, auditors' fees, accounting services, etc. *Not:* research, manufacturing, sales or distribution expenses.

Amortisation. Depreciation.

Appropriation account. Statement of accumulated profit.

Asset. Something owned by the business which has a measurable cost. Fixed, current or other assets.

Authorised capital. Share capital of the business authorised by law. May be only partly issued for cash. Ordinary or preference.

Bad debt. Debtor who fails to pay. Amount written off to expense.

Balance. Difference between the debits and credits in a ledger account.

Balance sheet. Accounting report. Statement of assets owned by a business and the way they are financed from liabilities and owners' equity. Does *not* indicate the market value of the business.

Bonds. Debentures. Long-term loans. Often secured on the assets. *Not* current liabilities.

Bookkeeping. Recording of transactions in debits and credits. Posting of transactions from journals to ledgers to provide data for accounting reports.

Book value. Two meanings: (a) Value of assets in the books (b) Value of ordinary shares in the books. Computed: owners' equity less preference shares, divided by the number of ordinary shares.

Buildings. Fixed assets unless acquired for resale. Depreciated to expense over its working life. Balance sheet value at cost less depreciation. Most market value sometimes revalued periodically. Land is *not* depreciated.

Capital. Capital surplus. Capital profit. *Not* available for normal dividend. *Not* accumulated profit. Includes share premium. *Not* cash.

Capital stock. Share capital in units of £100.

Capital surplus. Capital reserve.

Cash. Money asset of a business. Includes both cash in hand and cash at bank. Balance sheet current asset.

Cash discount. Discount allowed to a debtor for early payment of the debt. Terms may be: '2 and one half % for payment within 10 days or net (no discount) for payment within one month'.

Cash transaction. Receipt or payment of cash.

Claims. Claims against the assets of business. Owners or creditors. Total claims equal total assets. Creditors' claims are called liabilities. Owners' claims are called owners' equity.

Closing stock (inventory). Inventory at end of the accounting period. Part of the computation of cost of goods sold.

Collateral. Security.

Common stock. Ordinary stock.

Comparability. Accounting concept. Accounting reports are prepared consistently so that the data is comparable.

Company. Legal entity. Limited or unlimited. Regulated by the Companies Act 1948.

Consistency. Accounting concept. See comparability.

Conservatism. Accounting concept. Accounting reports avoid overstating the financial position. Profits usually not recognised as soon as they are known.

Contingent liability. Liability not yet recorded on the balance sheet which may or may not arise.

Convention. Assumption made in accounting. Many accounting concepts arise from assumptions that have proved to be practicable.

Corporation. Company.

Cost. Several meanings: (a) Expenditure on a given thing. (b) To compute the cost of something. (c) Direct cost or indirect cost (indirect cost is overhead, direct cost is part of goods sold)

Cost accounting. Recording of cost data and preparation of cost statements.

Cost concept. Accounting concept. Assets valued at cost *not* market value. Exceptions: (a) Fixed assets valued at cost less depreciation. (b) Current assets normally valued at the *lower* of cost or market value.

Cost of goods sold. Cost of goods *actually* sold during the accounting period. Excludes cost of goods left unsold. Excludes all overhead except manufacturing expenses. Charged in the income statement. Sales less cost of goods sold equals gross profit. Cost of sales.

Cost of sales. Cost of goods sold.

Creditor. Payable. Account payable. Liability. Money owed to other parties. Not owners' equity. Current or long-term liability.

Creditors' claims. Liabilities. *Not* owners' equity.

Credit transaction. Transaction which incurs, (accrues) liability. No cash is paid or received until later.

Cumulative preference shares. Preference shares whose unpaid dividends accumulate until they are eventually paid by the company. Some preference shares are specifically non-cumulative.

Current assets. Assets which are normally realised in cash or used up in operations during one operating period. Normally one year. Includes: cash, debtors, inventory, prepaid expenses. Not fixed or 'other' assets.

Current liability. Liability due for payment within one operating period, normally one year. Does not include: long-term liabilities or owners' equity.

Current tax liability. Current liability for income tax. Due within one year. See also future income tax liability.

Current ratio. Ratio of current assets to current liabilities. Measure of liquidity.

Debtor. Receivable, account receivable. Money due to business. Current asset.

Deferred shares. Shares of a company ranking for dividend after preference and ordinary shares. Deferred stock.

Deferred income. Income received in advance of being earned and recognised. Normally left as a theoretical current liability in the balance sheet, until the sale is made and the income recognised.

Deferred stock. Deferred shares.

Depreciation (buildings, vehicles, etc). Allocation of the cost of a fixed asset to expense over its working life. Measure of the *cost* of using the fixed asset. Land does not depreciate. See also accumulated depreciation, depreciation expenses, straight line depreciation and diminishing balance depreciation.

Depreciation expense. Depreciation (at cost) during the accounting period. *Not* the same as accumulated depreciation except in the first year of the fixed asset. See depreciation.

Diminishing balance depreciation. Depreciation method charging off the cost of a fixed asset by *level percentage* of the reducing balance over its working life. The percentage remains the *same* but the depreciation charge decreases.

Director. Officer of a limited company. Member of the board of directors. *Not* a partner.

Dual aspect. Accounting concept. Two aspects of each transaction. Basis of double entry bookkeeping. Debit and credit.

Earnings. Income. Profits. Revenues.

Entity. Accounting concept. Accounting reports are prepared for a *specific entity.* A shopkeeper who *personally* owns his business premises, has three entities and rewards:

Entity	*Reward*
Business/owner	Profit
Landlord	Rent
Employee	Wages

Equipment. Fixed asset if acquired for *long term use* and *not* for resale. Recorded in the balance sheet at cost less depreciation. Not at market value.

Expenditure. Money paid for cost, expense, asset or other purposes.

Expense. Expenditure properly chargeable in the income statement. Amount used up during the accounting period. Indirect cost. Manufacturing, selling or administrative expense. Includes *depreciation* of fixed assets. Expenses are 'matched' against revenues during the accounting period to compute the figure of profit. Not fixed asset.

Note: Purchases of small low value fixed assets (e.g. under £5 each) are often charged as expense, to avoid depreciation calculations and show a conservative financial position.

Face value. Nominal value of shares. Not the book (owners' equity) value or market value.

Fixed assets. Assets such as land, plant and equipment, acquired for long-term *use* in the business and *not* for resale. Charged to overhead periodically as *depreciation.* Recorded in the balance sheet at cost less depreciation, not market value. Sometimes revalued periodically. Land is *not* depreciated. See also expense.

Fixtures and fittings. Fixed assets if acquired for use and not for resale.

Furniture and fixtures. Fixed assets if acquired for use and not for resale.

Future tax liability. Reserve for future income tax. Tax computed on the current year's profit not due for payment until a future date. Normally becomes the current tax liability in the following year.

General expense. Expense of the business which is *not* part of goods sold, selling or administrative expense. Sometimes grouped with administrative expense in the income statement. Includes: auditors' fees, legal expenses, etc.

General reserve. Part of accumulated profits set aside in the owners' equity section of the balance sheet. Avoids distribution of profits as dividends. Is not an asset; is not cash. Merely part of owners' equity shown separately on the claims side of the balance sheet.

Going concern. Accounting concept. All accounting reports and values assume that the business is continuing and not about to liquidate (end). Accounting market values are therefore based upon those expected in the normal course of business.

Goodwill. Value of the name, reputation or intangible assets of a business. In accounting it is only recorded at cost when it is *purchased.* Not depreciated. Often written off to nil. Never valued at market price. Generally a hidden asset of a business.

Gross profit. Difference between sales and cost of goods sold. Profit computed before charging for selling and administrative expenses, etc.

Gross profit percentage. Measure of profitability computed:

$$\frac{\text{Gross Profit}}{\text{Net Sales}} \times 100\%$$

Income. Earnings. Profit. Revenue. Sometimes used to mean sales and all forms of incoming benefits. Not necessarily in cash.

Income statement. Profit and loss account. Earnings statement.

Income tax liability. See current tax liability or future tax liability.

Incomplete transaction. Transaction is incomplete at the end of the accounting period. Cause of uncertainty in accounting. Concept of profit recognition must be employed to determine in which accounting period the profit is earned.

Intangible asset. Asset which cannot be actually touched. Normally 'other' assets. *Not* fixed or current assets.

Investment. Amount invested in stocks, shares, bonds, debentures or any asset. See also trade investments and marketable securities.

Inventory. Stock of goods on hand for resale. Includes stores and supplies. Valued at cost or lower market value, not selling prices. Increased by purchases. Decreased by cost of goods sold. Balance sheet current asset. Not a fixed asset.

Issue capital. Share capital actually issued by a company. Part of owners' equity in the balance sheet. See also authorised capital. Price at which a share is first sold by a company.

Normally the nominal value plus share premium or less *share* discount. May be ordinary preference or deferred shares. *Not* bonds or debentures. *Not* cash. *Not* working capital.

Land. Freehold or leasehold property owned by a business. Normally fixed asset. Recorded at cost. *Not* depreciated. Sometimes revalued to market value. Difference between cost and revaluation increased fixed assets and also capital reserves.

Limitations of accounting. Accounting reports show a limited period of a business because: (a) Some important facts cannot be stated in money. (b) Accounting periods at fixed intervals create uncertainty from incomplete transactions. (c) Accounting *not* scientific but depends on judgement. (d) Accounting reports depend on concepts.

Limited company. Company whose shareholders have limited their liability to the amounts they subscribe to the shares they hold. Regulated by the Companies' Act 1948.

Long-term liability. Liability *not* due for payment within one year. Bonds, debentures or loans. Holders are creditors and receive interest. They are *not* shareholders. *Not* current liability. *Not* owners' equity.

Loss. Opposite of profit or income. Excess of costs and expenses over sales. Reduces owners' equity. May *not* affect the cash balance.

Loss or disposal of fixed assets. Loss due to sale or disposal of fixed assets. Excess of fixed asset cost over: accumulated depreciation, and scrap or sales proceeds. Treated as 'Other income and expense' in the statement.

Machinery. Fixed asset if acquired for use and *not* for resale. Valued at cost less depreciation. If produced or acquired for resale it becomes stock. See depreciation.

Maintenance cost. Expense of maintaining or repairing the fixed assets of the business. Charged as expense in the income statement.

Matching. Accounting concept. Costs and revenues in the accounting period should be 'matched' in order that the computed profit may be true and fair. Matching means 'appropriate to' not 'equal to'.

Money. Accounting concept. Limitation of accounting reports in that they do not reveal facts about the business which cannot be immediately expressed in money terms.

Manufacturing expenses. Overheads for manufacture. part of cost of goods sold. Not sales and administrative expense.

Mortgage. Long-term loan normally *secured* on a fixed asset liability. *Not* a current liability.

Net. Two meanings: (a) Figure after deduction, e.g. *gross* sales less sales returns equals *net* sales. (b) Payment of the full amount with no allowance for cash discount (2 and one half % 10 days, net 30 days).

Net profit. Profit for the accounting period after income tax. Income. Earnings. Increases owners' equity. Does *not* necessarily affect cash balance.

Net profit percentages. Measures of profitability: (a) Net profit to sales:

$$\frac{\text{Net profit}}{\text{Net sales}} \times 100\%$$

(b) Net profit to owners' equity return on investment

$$\frac{\text{Net profit}}{\text{Owners' equity}} \times 100\%$$

Note: This return on investment may appear to be high if the assets in the balance are significantly *undervalued.*

Net worth. Owners' equity. Balance sheet value of owners' claims based on the special accounting values. Does not indicate market value of a business.

Nominal value. Face value of shares. The authorised and issued share capital in the balance sheet shows the nominal values of the shares separately from any premiums or discount.

Not the full book value or market value.

Non operating expense. Expense which does not directly relate to *normal* operations. Loss on sale of fixed assets, interest paid, etc.

Non operating income. Income not arising from *normal* operations. Profit on sale of fixed assets, dividends received etc.

Notes to financial statements. Notes attached to the balance sheet and income statement which explain: (a) Significant accounting adjustments. (b) Information required by law if not disclosed in the financial statements. (c) Changes in accounting concepts used to prepare the financial statement.

Opening stock. Inventory at the beginning of the accounting period.

Operating cost. Operating expense.

Operating expenses. Overheads of the business. Sometimes restricted to selling, administrative and general expenses.

Operating profit. Gross profit less operating expense in the income statement.

Ordinary shares. Share capital. *Part* of owners' equity in the balance sheet. Holders entitled to dividends recommended by the directors. Not preference shares. Possible values: (a) Face or nominal values. (b) Market value. (c) Issue price (including any premium). (d) Book value (total owners' equity less the nominal value of preference shares). See also deferred shares.

Ordinary stock. Ordinary shares. Common stock. In units of £100.

Order. Purchase order to a supplier for delivery of goods and services.

Other assets. Assets which are *not* fixed or current assets. Normally: goodwill, research expenditure carried forward, trade investments, etc. Valued at cost not market value unless losses are exceptional.

Other creditors. Creditors for accruals are services not trade creditors for purchase of materials and supplies. Current liabilities.

Overhead. Overhead expense. Indirect cost which cannot be conveniently associated with a unit of production.

Overhead expenses. Overhead. Indirect cost. Fixed or variable with volume of production. See manufacturing sales and administrative or general expenses. *Not* direct cost. *Not* direct labour. *Not* direct material.

Owner's claims. Owners' equity.

Owner's equity. Owners' claims. Net worth. Amount due to owners of the business. Increased by profits. Reduced by losses and dividends. Note: Assets less liabilities equal owners' equity.

Package of accounting reports. Set of financial statements. Balance sheet, income statement, statement of accumulated profit.

Patent. Legal right to exploit an invention. Asset in the balance sheet. Recorded at cost less depreciation under the heading 'other assets'.

Payable. Creditor. Liability. Accounts payable.

Plant. Equipment and machinery. Fixed asset if acquired for use and *not* for resale.

Preference share. Share which entitles the holder to fixed dividends (only) in preference to the dividends for ordinary shares on liquidation. Normally entitled only to the nominal value. *No* right to share in excess profits. Preference stock.

Preference stock. Preference shares in units of £100.

Prepaid expense. Expense paid in advance for more than one accounting period.

Principles of accounting. Accounting concepts.

Profit. Income. Earnings. Excess of sales over costs and expenses, during an accounting period. Does not necessarily increase cash—it may be reflected in increased assets or decreased liabilities. Increases owners' equity. The term *net* profit sometimes means profit less income tax.

Profit after tax. Net profit. Profit before tax, less income tax for the accounting period, in the income statement.

Profit before tax. Operating profit less non-operating expenses plus non operating income, in the income statement.

Profit and loss account. Income statement. *Not* a balance sheet. Statement showing sales, costs, expenses and profit for an accounting period.

Profit and loss appropriation account. Statement of accumulated profit. Retained earnings. Balance of profit and loss account.

Provision. Several different meanings: (a) Reserve, i.e. future income tax liability. (b) Accumulation, i.e. accumulated depreciation. (c) Expense, i.e. depreciation expense. (d) Accrual, i.e. accrued expense liability.

Provision for income tax. Income tax on the profit in the income statement. Sometimes refers to: (a) The charge in the income statement and/or (b) The liability in the balance sheet.

Published financial statements. Balance sheet, profit and loss account and statement of accumulated profit, with comparative figures and notes disclosing the information required under the Companies' Act 1948. Less informative than internal statements. See notes to financial statement.

R and D. Research and development costs. Normally expense. Sometimes treated as 'other asset'.

Receivables. Accounts receivable. Debtors. Current assets.

Recognition of profit. Accounting concept. Profit is not

recognised and recorded until *realised* (in cash or debtors). Contrast losses which are recognised immediately they are known. Profit normally recognised when goods are shipped to the customer *not* when the order is received or when the customer pays for the goods.

Redeemable preference shares. Preference shares which may be re-purchased by the company from the shareholders. Part of owners' equity. *Not* ordinary shares.

Research cost. Cost of research. Separate overhead or part of manufacturing overhead. Expense. Sometimes carried forward as an 'Other asset' if it is of specific future benefit for a future limited period.

Retained earnings. Accumulated profits. Available for dividend. *Not* capital reserves. *Not* capital surplus. Part of owners' equity.

Returns. See sales returns.

Revenue. Earnings. Income. Profit. Sometimes also used to mean sales.

Revenue reserve. Profits available for dividend. Accumulated profit and general reserve. Retained earnings. *Not* capital reserve.

Rules. Accounting rules are concepts. Some rules are definite, others depend on judgement.

Sale. Price for which goods are sold. Total of amounts sold. Recognised normally when goods are shipped to the customer.

Sales allowance. Special allowance to a customer against the amount due for goods sold. Often allowed for damaged goods or shortages.

Sales discount. Trade or cash discount on sales.

Sales expense. Cost of promoting sales and retaining custom. Indirect cost. Overhead expense. *Not* manufacturing, administrative or general expense. Includes: advertising, sales literature, sales salaries, travelling expenses, depreciation of sales cars etc.

Sales return. Goods returned to a business by its customers.

Security. Collateral. Assets claimable in priority by some creditors to others.

Selling expense. Sales expense.

Share capital. Capital stock. Part of owners' equity. Money put into a business by the owners. Ordinary preference or deferred shares.

Shareholder. Stockholder. Owner of part of the share capital and owners' equity.

Share premium. Excess of original sales price of a share over its face or nominal value. Owners' equity. Capital reserve. *Not* available for dividend.

Shares. Document certifying ownership of shares in a company. Share capital. Part of owners' equity.

Stock. Inventory of goods on hand for resale. Stores. Raw material, work in process, finished goods. Valued at the lower of manufacturing cost or market value.

Stockholder. Shareholder.

Stock purchases. Purchases of goods for resale.

Stores. Stock supplies.

Straight line depreciation. Depreciation method charging off the cost of a fixed asset equally over the years of its working life. See also depreciation and diminishing balance depreciation.

Supplies. Materials used up but *not* part of the product.

Tangible asset. Asset which can be physically identified or touched. Sometimes means only those assets which have a definite value, i.e. excludes intangible assets, goodwill and R. and D. expenditures carried forward.

Trade creditor. Account payable. Money owed for credit purchases. Current liability.

Trade discount. Deduction from the selling price of an invoice because the buyer is in the same trade as the seller. *Not* a cash discount.

Trade investment. Investment in shares or debentures of another company in the same trade or industry. Long-term investment. *Not* a marketable security. 'Other asset' in the balance sheet. Valued at cost. Unless there is a substantial loss.

Transaction. Change in two items in the balance sheet. Cash or credit transaction. May be for sale, purchase, cash receipt, cash payment, or accounting adjustment. Translated into debits and credits in the bookkeeping records.

True and fair. Accounting concept. Balance sheet and income statement seek to show a 'true and fair' view of the business.

Uncertainty. A limitation of accounting uncertainty at the end of each accounting period makes it difficult to determine the true and fair position. This uncertainty arises from (a) incomplete transactions. (b) the market value of inventory. (c) working life of fixed assets for depreciation calculation. (d) realisable values of current assets. (e) contingent liabilities not yet known or calculable.

Unpaid dividends. Dividends declared as due to shareholders but *not* yet paid in cash. Shown as current liabilities in the balance sheet. Deducted from accumulated profits in the owners equity.

Value. Several meanings: (a) Accounting value—value according to accounting concepts, appropriate to the particular asset. Fixed assets valued at cost less depreciation. Current assets generally valued at cost or lower realisable value. (b) Market value—realisable value of inventory in the normal course of business. (Not in liquidation). (c) Real value—not known in accounting.

Working capital. Special meaning: Current assets less current liabilities. *Not* the same as 'capital'.

Working capital ratio. Ratio of current assets to current liabilities. Indication of the liquidity of the business.

Work in process. Inventory stock. Work partially completed. Valued at the lower of manufacturing cost or market value.

4 The marketing systems audit

'Prepare no plans or proposals simply if a way can be found to make them complex and wonderful.'

Ralph Murphy's Rule No. 1

The most common reaction we receive, when we indicate that we would like to review the marketing systems within a company, is one of astonishment coupled with non-comprehension. Despite this reaction, auditing the company marketing systems continues to be a vital step in understanding the true performance and situation of the total business.

The marketing system audit should cover:

The marketing and sales organisation.
The marketing information system.
The marketing planning system.
The marketing control system.
The new product development system.

It can be seen from the subject matter that the audit is almost purely internal and essentially concentrates on techniques, procedures and controls exercised by the senior marketing manager. It is the internal environment within which people conduct their work. Its objective is to both survey and analyse the scope and effectiveness of the systems in use. From the results we not only obtain insight and understanding of the method and style of the business, we also gain indications as to the areas on which we should paticularly concentrate as we complete the remaining sections of the audit.

The marketing systems audit should not consume a disproportionate amount of time. If you work with a prepared questionnaire, which is specific to the business, it can be completed both efficiently and quickly.

The marketing organisaton

Marketing people seem to love organisation charts. Perhaps some basic, unsatisfied need, buried in our subconscious mind, is satisfied through drawing boxes and connecting them with lines. Putting initials and abbreviated position titles into the boxes appears to be the ultimate degree of satisfaction. The preoccupation with boxes and lines often precludes any real understanding of the organisation structure, its efficiency and effectiveness, and its role within the total business.

The purpose of the organisation structure should be to arrange and relate the work to be performed so that it can be accomplished, most effectively, by the people resources available. The structure should also:

Develop as the work to be performed develops.
Establish clear and understood authority, responsibilities and individual accountability.
Establish relationships and mutually cooperative efforts of the people for the good of the company.

In practice we find the structure very rarely reflects these criteria.

In auditing the structure, whatever the size or nature of the business, we have found that, by simply obtaining answers to the following questions, we can very quickly obtain the necessary understanding of the structure's efficiency and effectiveness. At the same time it also enables us to make the necessary recommendations and changes to improve the situation.

1. Organisation chart
Is there a published organisation chart for the total business?

Is there a published organisation chart for the marketing department?
Do the people who appear on both charts have copies of the charts?
Are the position titles understood by one and all?
Are they clear to you?

2. Structure development

How long has the structure been in place?
Why was it changed?
Does the structure appear to be based on the work to be performed or the people available?
Is it regularly reviewed and if so, what were the conclusions of the last review?
Are lines of communications clearly established and do they work in practice?
Does the structure operate in practice in accordance with the published chart?
Do the people involved believe the structure works in practice?

3. Job responsibility

Are job specifications or position charts published for each position in the marketing department?
Do they relate to the actual work being done?
Do all managers have copies of everyone else's job specifications?
Do the job specifications contain clear guidelines on authority and responsibility of the position in question?
Do the authorities and responsibilities work in practice?
Are individuals really held accountable for what they are supposed to be accountable for?
How often are job specifications reviewed and what were the results of the last review?
Are the critical aspects of authority, responsibility and accountability understood by the necessary managers outside the marketing department?

4. Organisation efficiency and effectiveness

Do you get the feeling that the structure is really designed to

satisfy individuals' needs rather than reflecting the work to be done?
What and where are the organisational conflicts and relationship problems?
What improvements do the *people* believe could improve efficiency and effectiveness?
Does everyone *really* have a job to do?

Now, obviously you cannot walk into the marketing director's office and run through the questions as though you were a researcher conducting an attitude survey. You clearly need to use your discretion in questioning and observing every member of the organisation to obtain the necessary input to answer the questions. The senior marketing man may tell you that everyone understands and works to agreed job specifications. Talking to his product manager, it becomes clear that he not only cannot find his job specification but that he really does not know what was in it—if that really mattered at all. Experience enables you to identify the problems quickly.

Within our experience of evaluating and analysing organisations two comments seem regularly to be applicable. First, organisation structures tend never to operate the way they were intended to. Secondly, they tend to reflect the style and approach of the ultimate boss, be he president, general manager, or vice-president in charge. If the latter is true, then the structure can be a disaster, often reflecting the pure ego satisfaction needs of the gentleman in the top box, the structure itself bearing no theoretical or practical relationship to the work that has to be performed.

Perhaps the most important words of advice we can give to anyone auditing the organisation are:

Do not believe what people tell you—believe what you see.
Beware of the manager who says, 'I can tell you everything you need to know'.
Ego is a common characteristic yet disastrous within, and for, business.

The marketing information system

Lord Kelvin once said:

> 'When you can measure what you are speaking about and express it in numbers, you know something about it; or when you cannot measure it, when you cannot express it in numbers, your knowledge is of a meagre and unsatisfactory kind. It may be the beginning of knowledge, but you have scarcely in your thought advanced to the stage of a science.'

This still remains the most apt introduction to information systems, whatever their orientation. It has often been stated that business involves the management of five resources: money, materials, machines, people and information.

Much management time and resources are allocated to the first four activities. They are regularly analysed, reviewed, and changed. Rarely, however, do we find adequate time and resources allocated to the fifth resource—information. Yet to every functional activity of the business it is vitally important, and none more so than marketing. With so much of the activity of marketing decision making being qualification, an effective information system becomes essential.

Obviously one of the first things to look for is evidence of any form of formal information system. However, we think it is fair to say that, with the advent of relatively low cost computer systems and programmes, there tends to be an abundance of information in most companies. Regretfully this information very often suffers from:

Being voluminous and of the wrong kind.
Being sparse when it comes to the right kind.
Being totally dispersed throughout the company, to the point that even simple facts are difficult to locate or confirm.
Being suppressed or hidden by certain individuals in the mistaken belief that the information may reflect unfavourably on their position or performance.
Important information arriving too late or going to the wrong people.

Unimportant information always arriving on time.
The information often arriving in a format that is unusable and requires much time and effort to convert it into a usable format.
The information arriving in a form that gives no indication as to whether it is fact or opinion.

The real objective of any information system must be to provide timely, accurate and interpretative facts and opinions to aid the decision making process. To accomplish this objective, the information system should first be formal, secondly regularly assessed in terms of accuracy and thirdly regularly reviewed as to its reliability and use. It is specifically these points, plus the usual symptoms mentioned earlier, that should be reviewed and anlaysed. The lack of information is more readily identifiable than the excess of useless information. When faced with determining what information is *really* required, then posing the question, 'Do I receive this information because it is nice to know or because I need to know in order to perform my job?' gives us the answer. Shelves and cupboards full of computer tab runs and senior managers who know the excess inventory in some obscure and unimportant subsidiary indicate that the wrong information is being given to the wrong person. A marketing manager who does not know his product's contribution year to date, is clearly suffering from a distinct lack of the right information.

Very often we find that the audit of the control systems gives us valuable insight into the effectiveness of the information system.

The marketing planning system

In many companies the formalisation of the planning system, whether it be marketing planning or business planning, has developed into almost a means unto itself. The objective seems to be planning, with the standards being the satisfaction of some corporate or higher body. Whilst marketing planning cannot exist in isolation and we accept it cannot exist without the establishment of corporate objectives and standards, it must not be solely organised to satisfy an internal need.

The planning system should be formalised and at the same time recognise the need to change and update plans as the implementation date gets closer. The audit of the planning system (remember at this stage we are auditing the system, not the content of the plans) is relatively straightforward. We are looking for:

A formalised planning cycle of timings, events and responsibilities.
Effective overall control of the planning cycle.
Progress reviews as the planning is implemented.
Pre-determined control points.
Corrective action based on comparison of actual performances against plan.
Adequate timings for completion of meaningful plans.

Very often one finds that, following a fast review of what material is available on planning, it becomes abundantly clear that the system being used falls into one of the following categories:

The system is highly formalised and detailed, but in practice appears to be satisfying internal management needs rather than the overall business needs. Managers plan what they think senior management wants to see, in both quality and quantity.
The system is highly formalised and detailed but in practice is not followed nor completed with any degree of accuracy.
No real system exists, the future really being determined by one senior person in the organisation who may utilise the opinions of some of his managers. He makes commitments only when circumstances force him to do so.

However we feel that over the last few years, in both Europe and North America, the practical approach which companies take towards planning has improved tremendously. the advent of the computer, used in a practical way, offers management an effective tool with which to improve the many quantitative forecasts in which they are involved.

Within the total area of the marketing planning system the two most difficult areas to audit are undoubtedly: Forecasting techniques and Development of objectives and strategies. In many cases we find a good overall planning system in use, with sufficient detail, time allocation and functional management involvement, but it becomes an ineffective system because of the poor quality of the forecasting and the technique and relevance of the objective and strategy development process.

Forecasting

Over the years we have come across every possible type of forecasting technique, from basic intuition of the man in charge to sophisticated computer models. There is no summary statement which specifies the right or best method to use. There is no forecast which will consistently be accurate. Of the alternatives open to use we must judge both the techniques and their relevance to the business before we start the forecasting process. Overall, we like to use a rule of thumb approach, before we get into the details, which looks at the cost of the forecasting process (in terms of management time, computer time, outside services, research, etc.) against the cost to the company of inaccurate forecasting. This gives us the first evaluation of the relevance of the process to the practical requirement of the business. If the business is such that it is totally flexible in coping with the volume differences, then spending fortunes on computerised forecasting systems seems somewhat of an overkill.

As we then get into the elements of the forecasting system we basically are looking for the degree of relevance to the particular business. The key points to look for are the following:

1. Time frames of forecasts

Is there just one global forecast or is there a systematic

breakdown of the forecast, based on different time frames?
Immediate: One to three months—for operational control.
Short term: three to twelve months—scheduling, departmental planning, purchasing, etc.
Medium term: one to three years — resource allocation, investments.
Long term: three to ten years — strategic planning.

2. Scope of forecasting

Total market — by product
— by area
— by market segment
Company sales — by product
— by area
— by market segment
— by specific time frame
Resource requirements and their costs.
Alternative predictions and their effect on forecasted figures.

3. Use of forecasts

Which functional departments use the forecast?
What is the purpose and how do they use it?
Is the forecast done in a manner and format that makes it easy to use?

4. The forecast's 'fit' to corporate goals

Does the forecast take into account the corporate agreed objectives?
Does the forecast recognise and reflect the corporate constraints of men, money, materials and time?
Is the forecast achievable within the resource guidelines laid down by the corporation?

As we said earlier, the actual techniques being used by companies vary greatly and there is no magic formula for the right techniques. If you really are unsure as to whether the technique is the right one for the business, a good way of judging is to go back over historical forecasts, say the last two years, and measure actual results against a particular forecast. At least you can then have an objective judgement as to the accuracy of the technique being used. But remember it is unlikely that any forecasting technique will be one hundred per cent accurate, but a one hundred per cent variance to forecast is at the same time not acceptable.

Development of objectives and strategies

Objectives and strategies seem to be one subject that causes utter confusion amongst most marketing people. It seems strange to us that, recognising the factor, few companies bother adequately to define objectives and strategies and ensure all key staff understand the definition. This always leads to the poor development of meaningful objectives and the resultant strategies. The simplest and best definitions we have found are:

Objective	'A significant goal to be achieved.'
Strategy	'Management of the mix of money, materials and people resources to achieve an agreed objective.'

In other words a strategy is the means you use to achieve a specified goal.

With the overall sequence of planning, the goals or objectives must clearly relate to some specified opportunity which has been identified. The resulting strategies should then specifically relate to the achievement of the objective. In practice it is often found that one particular strategy may be utilised to achieve more than one objective. For example, a strategy of raising prices by fifteen per cent could contribute towards the achievement of a sales volume objective, a gross margin objective, or a product mix volume objective.

In auditing the development of objectives and strategies, within the context of the marketing system part of the audit, we are looking for the logic and relationships between opportunities, objectives, and strategies, and not an evaluation of the rightness or effectiveness of them. That particular evaluation is covered under the chapters on elements of the marketing mix.

Unlike planning cycles and systems, objective and strategy development is very rarely formalised. In many cases the objectives are not quantified and the strategies being implemented are not even committed to paper. Having found many such situations, we developed a simple chart (Figure 4.1) which is completed for each objective. The chart is first completed from published documentation and further as a result of discussion with the specific marketing managers. This later stage picks up the strategies unpublished but, in practice, being implemented. The gaps in the final form give us strong indications as to the effectiveness of the development process being used. Because marketing people are so often confused by this subject, with the result that the documented statements are all over the place, unrelated or finally not even committed in writing, a formalised layout of their objectives can be a great aid to understanding. For the marketing auditor the fastest way to get an understanding of the company's objectives and strategies is often to restate the written and unwritten word in this formalised format. It always seems to throw up the weaknesses immediately.

Following the objectives and strategies are the development stages of:

The specific programmes.
Work schedules.
Formulation of budgets.

The specific programmes are the tactical documents (Table 4.1) which serve as working bibles for the implementation process. The work schedules detail who does what and when it should be done by. They should be reviewed in terms of their detail, content and practicability. As you can imagine, we favour a fairly formalised approach to this, thus ensuring we do not miss the detail but more importantly that everyone

Figure 4.1 Planning strategies

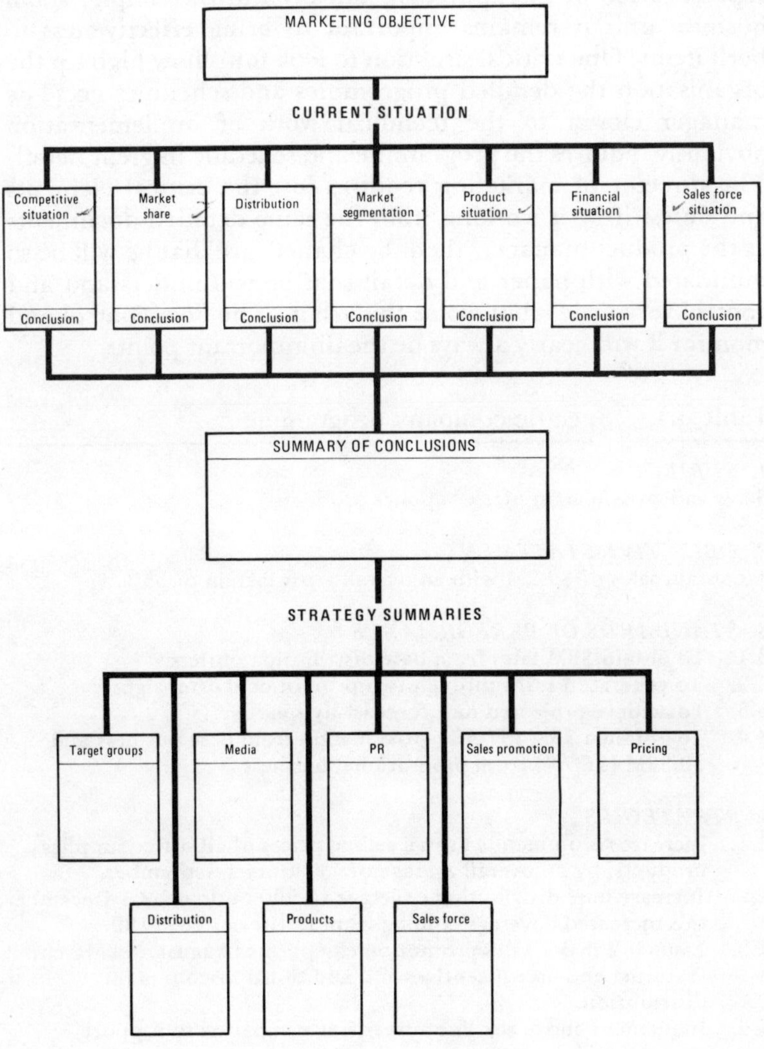

understands precisely what is expected of them. The complexity and size of the business will determine the sophistication of the approach, but even in the simple, small business unit it remains important to bring effectiveness to both items. One critical situation to look for is how high up the organisation the detailed programmes and schedules go. The manager closest to the technical work of implementation obviously requires the programme and schedule in great detail. The director of marketing requires just the critical elements and dates; if he is working from the same detailed documents as the product manager, then the chances are that he will be so inundated with paper and detail that he will understand and control very little—but worse than that, if he does control and monitor it will nearly always be the unimportant points.

Table 4.1. Specific company programme

1. SUBJECT
Sales and gross margin office supplies products

2. OBJECTIVE STATEMENT
To obtain sales of $9.2M with an overall gross margin of 35%.

3. STANDARDS OF PERFORMANCE
3.1. To obtain $8M sales from base distribution outlets.
3.2. To generate $1.2M through two promotional campaigns
3.3. To achieve projected unit forecast by quarter.
3.4. To obtain a $3M (37.5%) gross margin from base business and $0.32M (26.7%) from promotional business.

4. STRATEGIES
4.1. Increase recommended retail selling prices of all office supplies products, by an overall average of 7%, from 1 September.
4.2. Increase base distribution coverage to 500 outlets, by 1 December, this increased coverage coming from territories 187+189.
4.3. Launch 2 major sales promotion campaigns (August and March) featuring end-user incentives and additional discounts for distribution.
4.4. Implement above the line advertising campaigns to support promotional campaigns.
4.5. New collateral literature to be produced and direct mailed to all existing distribution channels.

5. *BACKGROUND RATIONALE*
   Whilst unit sales are only growing at +/– 5% per annum, the market is now projected to decline next year. This can be partially offset by price increases, without affecting volume. Our distribution coverage is satisfactory with the exception of the South-west. Our non-promotional business has been very steady at $+/– 7.5M, but promotional business has suffered through poorly conceived and executed campaigns. With the right support we should double this business.

6. *FINANCIAL CONSIDERATIONS ('000's omitted)*

Additional sales volume	$1100
Additional gross margin	385
Additional expenditures directly related to increase sales and	
Advertising and SP	$ 120
Sales cost, incl. commission	55
Shipping and freight	110
TOTAL	$ 285
Additional contribution	$ 100

Marketing plans

It almost goes without saying that a formal marketing plan should be the end result of the complete marketing planning process. This document details the total process of planning, including the objectives, strategies, implementation programmes, budgets and schedules for the coming year. Overall we look at marketing plans in terms of:

Format used.
Degree of detail included in plan.
Circulation of the plan.
Practical use of the plan by marketing management.

The format will vary greatly depending on the business, but for everyone's ease of understanding a similar format should be used for all product lines. Completely different formats, for different product lines, make it very difficult for managers fully to utilise the marketing plans. Having been exposed to many formats we have come to the conclusion that whilst there is no standard marketing plan format that can be applied to all companies, as a minimum the format should include sections covering:

Industry and market analysis.
Competitive situation.
Market segmentation.
Product analysis.
Pricing analysis.
Sales force analysis.
Marketing communications analysis.
Historical sales, margin and contribution.
Progress against current objectives.
Projected opportunity analysis.
Objectives, strategies.
Campaign and promotional plans.
Budget.
Timings and event schedules.

In evaluating the format being used we tend to look for specific coverage of the above points, and if no reference is made to a specific item, then a valid explanation should be available.

The other surprising occurrence we often come across is that, having spent much time and effort completing the plan, it then has such a limited circulation that it almost defeats the objective of its production. Yes, the document is confidential, but it must as a minimum be available to all the managers who have an active part to play in implementing the plan details. It should also be available to the financial controller, manufacturing manager and advertising agency. Without the plan being in the hands of the right managers it will never stand a chance of being implemented to the full.

Assuming the published plan does receive the circulation it deserves, one then has to look for evidence of its use throughout the year. The marketing manager who has difficulty locating the whereabouts of his marketing plan is clearly not using it the way he should. The plan should really be the bible by which the marketing manager operates throughout the year.

It should be a document for:

Reference.
Guidance.
Quantification.
Qualification.
Control.

In many senses it is also the standard against which the manager's performance should be evaluated.

The marketing control system

In many cases auditing the marketing control systems gives inputs which aid your evaluation of the information and planning systems in operation. The control systems are essentially the techniques and review points which are formalised and followed through to ensure that when we delegate authority and responsibility we do not abdicate total accountability (see Figure 4.2). The degree of detail one has to go into will be very much dependent on the size and complexity of the business being audited. We have found that working from a master questionnaire is the best technique, thus ensuring that we do not miss anything important. A sample questionnaire is detailed in Table 4.2.

By weighting the questions with their importance to the specific business and at the same time rating the effectiveness of each item, it is not too difficult to quantify the effectiveness of the control systems.

New product development

Depending upon the particular business, new product development may well be outside the operations of the marketing department. If, however, it is the part of the marketing responsibility, it should be audited. In this case we are auditing

Table 4.2 Marketing system audit—control systems questionnaire

	Performance	Rating Factor
1. *Product controls*		
1.1. Are specific product and product groups units, $ sales and margins reported regularly?	1 2 3 4 5	
1.2. Do sales/margin reports go to the right managers?	1 2 3 4 5	
1.3. Are product line contribution reports produced regularly?	1 2 3 4 5	
1.4. Do they go to the right manager?	1 2 3 4 5	
(i) price reviews		
(ii) cost analysis		
(iii) promotions analysis		
(iv) product additions		
(v) product deletions		
(vi) product line item count growth	1 2 3 4 5	
2. *Pricing and cost controls*		
2.1. Are annual sales contracts reviewed regularly to determine the impact of cost changes?	1 2 3 4 5	
2.2. Are competitive pricing analyses and rationales available explaining differences?	1 2 3 4 5	
2.3. Are variances from list prices controlled by appropriate managers?	1 2 3 4 5	
2.4. Are special pricing arrangements, promotional prices, and 'deals' reported as variances from list prices?	1 2 3 4 5	
2.5. Does product/marketing management have detailed cost sheets (incl. labour, material, packaging, overheads, etc.) for all products?	1 2 3 4 5	
2.6. Is the standard cost system in use for projecting profits?	1 2 3 4 5	
2.7. Are these historical records on product pricing including % increases & decreases?	1 2 3 4 5	
2.8. Are prices compared country to country?	1 2 3 4 5	

3. *Receivables, credits, returns and inventory*

3.1.	Are receivables monitored by marketing management?	1 2 3 4 5
3.2.	Are credits/returns corrected and detailed on sales and margin reports?	1 2 3 4 5
3.3.	Are credits and returns monitored according to: (i) product and product lines? (ii) reason? (iii) authorised by management?	1 2 3 4 5
3.4.	Is there a formalised credit rating system?	1 2 3 4 5
3.5.	Is the credit rating of customers periodically reviewed?	1 2 3 4 5
3.6.	Are detailed inventory reports available to appropriate marketing management?	1 2 3 4 5
3.7.	Is inventory analysed by marketing in terms of on-going, excess, obsolete and related to short-term forecasted sales?	1 2 3 4 5

4. *Advertising*

4.1.	Is advertising expense planned and related to sales objectives?	1 2 3 4 5
4.2.	Is advertising formally evaluated in terms of: (i) effectiveness? (ii) cost performance vs plan?	1 2 3 4 5
4.3.	Is there a recognised and enforced monitoring procedure to monitor advertising costs related to advertising campaigns?	1 2 3 4 5

5. *Marketing plans*

5.1.	Is there a format marketing plan, by product line?	1 2 3 4 5
5.2.	Do all relevant managers have copies of the marketing plan?	1 2 3 4 5
5.3.	Is the marketing plan regularly used by managers?	1 2 3 4 5
5.4.	Does the senior marketing manager regularly review progress against plan with responsible manager?	1 2 3 4 5
5.5.	Are objectives reviewed as to its relevance on the year's progress?	1 2 3 4 5

the system of control, not the content or effectiveness of new product development programmes – that would be a functional audit of the specific department.

Because of the failure rate of new product ideas and the ultimate cost to the company, a formal control system must exist if management is to exercise any form of accountability for its investments in new product development. The system should be formalised and as a minimum cover the following stages:

Ideas gathering.
Ideas screening.
Concept development and testing.
Prototype development and testing.
Test marketing.
Full launch.

The controls at each stage should include (not necessarily in priority order):

Ultimate unit forecast.
Sales volume projections.
Margin projections.
Revised budgets for next development stage and for programme completion.
Actual expenditures to date versus budget.
Management evaluation and rating of possibility of ultimate development.

The biggest weaknesses we have seen in most companies are that:

The right controls and management involvement rarely occur in practice even though a formal 'system' may exist.
When projections change the right people are not informed.
The longer the development stage takes, the less practical interest the management takes in the project.

Over the years we have come across countless effective new product development control systems. It is indeed difficult, if not impossible, to say which is the best. Our view is that the

Figure 4.2 Control cycle

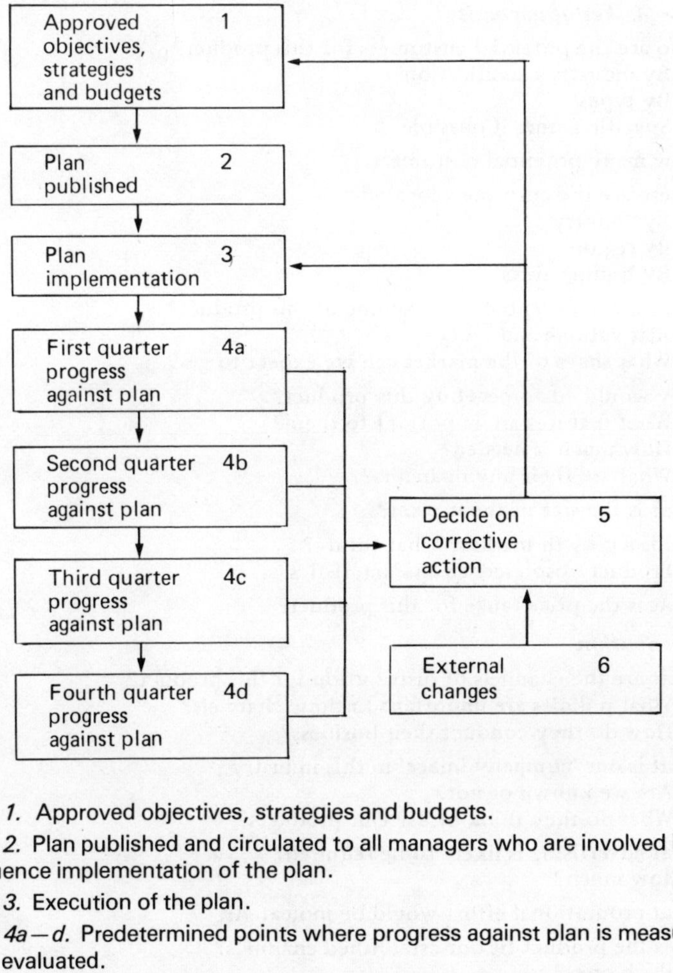

Box 1. Approved objectives, strategies and budgets.

Box 2. Plan published and circulated to all managers who are involved in or influence implementation of the plan.

Box 3. Execution of the plan.

Box 4a–d. Predetermined points where progress against plan is measured and evaluated.

Box 5. Decision made as to whether variances to plan warrant corrective action. Corrective action may be in the form of changing method of implementation to put performance back on plan or a basic change to either plan objectives or strategies because they are no longer valid.

Box 6. External changes may occur which also require alterations to plan implementation or objectives and strategies.

Table 4.3 Marketing checklist

The Market opportunity

Who are the potential customers for this product?
   By industry classification
   By types
   Specific names if possible

How many potential customers?

Where are the customers located?
   By country
   By region
   By trading areas

What is the potential sales volume of this product?
(Dollar volume and unit)
   What share of the market can we expect to get?

Why would customers buy this product?
   What features are important to them?
   How much is needed?
   What are their buying habits?

What is the size of the market?

Is this a growth market? What future?
   Product obsolescence characteristics.

What is the price range for this product?

Distribution

What are the channels of distribution for this product?
   What policies are important to these channels?
   How do they conduct their business?

What is our 'company image' in this industry?
   Are we known or not?
   What do they think of us? Our products?

What advertising is likely to be required?
   How much?

What promotional effort would be indicated?

Does the product fit our established channels?
   Which ones?
   Can it be handled without neglecting our present products?

Competition

What competition can we expect? (Companies and products)
   What is their 'image'?
   How do they sell? Policies, distribution, etc. . .?

(Any soft spots?)
Is the field overcrowded?

Can we expect to compete successfully with existing products?
Why?

Can the present products be quickly improved or can our product be easily copied?

Finance

Based on estimates from engineering,
What are GPs involved?
What return on investment?
What are P + L projections?
Cash flow.
Time to reach breakeven.
Long term profit outlook.

---

nature and size of the enterprise, and therefore its investments in new product development, should determine the type of control system used and the degree of detail into which it should go. As a yardstick, we show a minimum checklist (Figure 4.3, Tables 4.3 and 4.4) for evaluating such a system, recognising it may not be detailed enough, or in fact already too detailed.

Summary

Auditing the marketing systems is frequently not done at all, yet it is the internal environment within which all marketing activity takes place. As such, it influences not only the efficiency of the marketing department but also its effectiveness. Of all the specific areas of a complete marketing audit, the systems audit is both fairly standard in approach and does not vary by country, industry, size of company, etc.

As a minimum it should cover:

Organisation.
Information systems.
Planning systems.
Control systems.
New product development.

To both simplify and speed up the process, try to work from prepared checklists and questionnaires, but be flexible enough to go deeper than just the questionnaire if the situation demands it. Do not fall into the trap of completing the systems audit from the perspective of one individual: obtain the opinions of every key member of the marketing department. Provided you have done your homework correctly, do not be surprised, or think you have missed something, if the audit is completed in a day!

Table 4.4 Technical checklist

1. Patent problems or advantages.
2. Number of sizes and types.
3. Time to develop.
4. Cost to develop.
5. Problems in development.
6. Availability of engineering equipment and personnel.
7. Problems in manufacturing.
8. Problems of materials.
9. Rough estimate of capital required to put into production including tooling and facilities.
10. Rough estimates of costs and selling prices.
11. Time to absorb development costs.
12. Long-range prospects.
13. Possibility of establishing foothold on new technology.

Key audit points

1. Remember Murphy's Second Law:

   'It is usually impractical to worry beforehand about interference during system implementation; if you have none, someone will supply it for you.'

   Corollary 3 — the more innocuous a modification appears to be, the further its influence will extend and the more plans will have to be redrawn.

Figure 4.3 New product control sheet

Date ____________

____

____

STATUS

Preliminary Stage					*Specification Stage*
High	*Med.*	*Low*			
3	2	1	Probability of development		________ %
3	2	1	Probability of marketing		________ %
4	2	0	Size of market & competition	Estimated volume	________ Units (×)
4	2	0	Estimated profit	Estimated profit contr.	$________ (×)
1	2	3	Time required	Selling price ____ Cost ____	
1	2	3	Development costs (future)		$________ (+)
+					

Rating ______ (Date) ______ (Date)

STEPS: Things to be done

Comments	*Est. Time*	*Est. Expense*
Preliminary investigation:		
Specifications:		
Development:		
Field testing:		

PROGRESS REPORT:

Date	*Comments*

2. The organisation chart usually does not explain how the organisation really works.
3. Make sure you understand the work that has to be done before you evaluate the organisation structure.
4. Are the individual manager's responsibilities, authorities and accountabilities understood by himself and others?
5. Are job descriptions published for all management personnel?—are they distributed?
6. What do people think of the organisation structure and its effectiveness?
7. Is there a formal procedure for the flow of information through the company?
8. Is there too much information of the wrong kind? Conversely, too little information of the right kind?
9. Does the right information go to the right people at the right time?
10. Do managers get information because it is nice to know, or because they need to know?
11. Is there a formalised planning cycle and schedule in existence?
12. Is the planning approach followed in practice?
13. Is the forecasting technique being used practical and relative to the business needs?
14. Is the forecast detailed enough and do people use it?
15. What historical accuracy has there been on the forecast?
16. Are clear and understood objectives and strategies used?
17. Are they implemented?
18. Do they relate to the opportunity analysis?
19. Are they practical, quantified by standards—or simply 'motherhood and flag' statements?
20. Are the marketing plans being used and controlled on a regular basis?
21. Is the format complete and relative to the business?
22. Is there an organised control procedure for all elements of the plan?
23. Are the control points determined before or after the event?

24. Who is responsible for new product development?
25. Is the screening technique satisfactory?
26. Are costs evaluated at each stage of development?
27. Are the right managers involved in the decision making process?

5 Products, packaging, product costs

'Sir, we must beware of needless innovation, especially when guided by logic.'

W.S. Churchill

Introduction

A thorough knowledge of the company's products and their characteristics is fundamental to one's understanding of any business. Without products, after all, there is no business. This may seem an obvious point to make, yet many, many plans are conceived in partial ignorance of what is being offered. This is particularly true in the case of advertising plans. Frequently these are made by agency personnel with inadequate training. But even internal plans sometimes suffer from the lack of the right kind of product information.

Much has been written already about product management. The well-known theories have been covered time and time again. In most cases, however, the subject matter has considered only companies with a limited, well-defined or well-grouped range of products. Little attention has been paid to the average company, in our experience, with its dozens or even hundreds of products in various configurations. How does it all apply to them? What approach do we take here? In this chapter we will attempt to cover all types and sizes of companies.

Objectives of the product audit

Our principal aim is to gain a complete understanding of the product range, its characteristics, structure and performance which will enable us to draw sensible conclusions, make correct decisions and formulate profitable new strategies. We need to arrive at the best short- and long-term product strategies. We should also seek ways of increasing profitability through range rationalisation, cost reduction, product mix changes and a better application of marketing funds.

Product knowledge

The first, and most obvious, move in conducting a product audit is to look at the products themselves. All together. Even if you work directly or indirectly with the products every day it is useful once in a while to take a fresh, analytical look at them. Why together? Because this is the best, and quickest way of assessing the scale of the problem you are facing. It shows you the face you are projecting to the public: whether or not your image is one of quality; whether the range holds together visually or appears fragmented. You might also discover some products you had temporarily forgotten—this can easily happen in a multi-product company.

Your next requirement is a rationale for each product and group of products. How did each product originate? Where does each fit? What needs do they serve? What are the features, advantages and benefits for each product, (or product group where it is merely a matter of configurations)? All of these questions are very relevant and the answers to them should be properly documented. This very basic information usually indicates areas of weakness—in the products or in knowledge about them. It can also prove to be a very useful indicator towards product line rationalisation.

Quite recently we were involved in reorganising an old established company manufacturing a comparatively simple little product for use in industry. From the one basic product, however, their range had grown to over three hundred references. Fine, if sales had grown in anything like proportion. But they had not. This problem and possible solutions were identified in the first few minutes' examination of the range. Why were they needed? What benefits did each offer that could not have been satisfied by another? The answer that came out was that particular requirements of a few customers generated 'specials'; these specials were retained in the range; because they were there some sales were generated; so they were never eliminated. This is not an uncommon story; it happens in all kinds of companies for the same sort of reasons.

Packaging

At the time of examining the products it also makes sense to review packaging and packaging configurations. This assessment should take into account five factors:

The image projected.
Brand and/or corporate identity.
Whether or not it aids product positioning.
Whether or not the product is adequately protected.
The use made of shippers.

For good or bad, packaging projects an image of the brand on the company. Very often it is the consumer's or user's first point of contact. Whilst most people in the consumer products areas have already accepted this fact, it is often neglected in the commercial and industrial sectors where display packaging is not needed. But some form of packaging is necessary and this is usually seen by the user and the trade, so it makes sense even here to let it carry a message and an identity. If a package is to be printed anyway, it need not cost more to do the job properly.

Wherever possible, packaging should be bright, modern and in keeping with the target audience (see Chapter 6). Display packaging should obviously attract the eye. The brand name should be promoted clearly and the overall image projected must be consistent with all related advertising and sales promotional material. Packaging can, and should, give the product added value. It can also be a positive aid in product positioning, helping to differentiate clearly between one product and another.

The original purpose of packaging was to protect the product. To check whether the packaging fulfills this function well, one should examine the records of goods damaged in transit. A small percentage of complaints can be accepted as normal. An absence of complaints indicates that the goods are over-packaged and that cost savings can be made.

In our final examination of packaging we should look for potential cost saving areas. Simple questions can often result in economies. Does this pack really need to be so big? Could we use cheaper material? Do we really need four-colour printing? And so on.

It is always wise to check on the use of shipping cartons too. This is a common area of waste, usually because too many different sizes of carton are employed. This problem often starts with a product manager specifying packaging quantities which cannot be accommodated in an existing carton. Money can frequently be saved by standardising on a limited range of sizes and using fillers to make up any gaps. Also possible is a change in packaging quantities to achieve the same end.

Competition

An analysis of competition correspondingly starts with product knowledge. All competitive products must be carefully examined and tested. Their features, advantages and benefits should be documented and compared with our own. In particular we need an assessment of comparative quality, product versus product. And we need to obtain a clear understanding of their product positioning compared with ours. (Pricing, sales and distribution comparisons appear in the appropriate chapters of this book).

An interesting and very illustrative way of looking at relative positioning is through the use of positioning maps (see Figure 5.1). In this case we use the variables of price and quality but other combinations are possible and equally useful. The measurement of quality is, of course, partly judgmental unless some form of scoring system is devised against technical and sales features. In any case, the objective is more to give a feel of the relationship between products rather than to provide an absolute measurement.

Figure 5.1 Comparative price/quality display

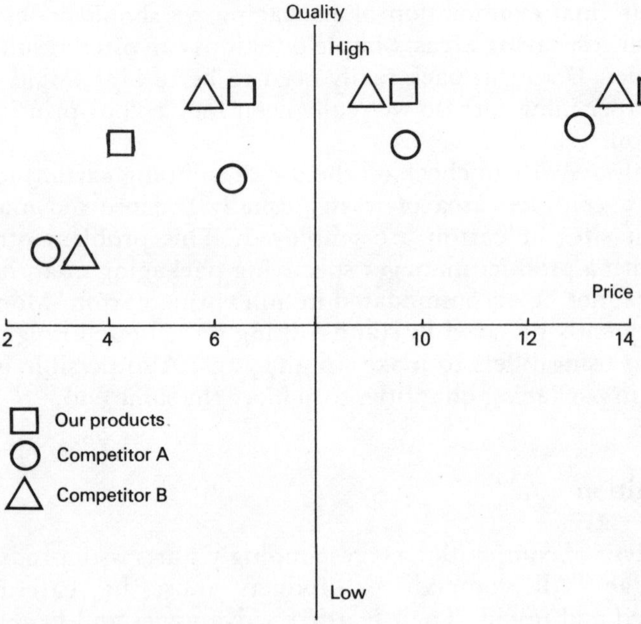

The strategic importance of a detailed knowledge of competition should not be underestimated. It is used as an aid in product positioning, in planning defensive or attacking strategies, and last but not least as the first step in identifying new product opportunities.

Market share

In the early 1970s the marketing experiences of a wide variety of US companies were channelled into a research project undertaken by the Marketing Science Institute in Cambridge, Massachusetts.* This study, known as PIMS (Profit Impact of Marketing Techniques), was based on original work carried out for the General Electric Company. The results were remarkable in their consistency and are now fairly well known. The computer model derived from this work makes it possible to predict, with a high degree of accuracy, profitability and return on investment resulting from changes in marketing strategy under specific market conditions.

Perhaps the most significant conclusion from the study was that profitability and return-on-investment (ROI) increase with market share. On average, businesses with market shares over thirty-six per cent produced returns on investment more than three times higher than businesses with shares of less than seven per cent. A further conclusion, however, proved that high product quality can partly offset a weak market position, i.e. a high quality product with a low market share achieves a similar ROI to a low quality product with a high share and considerably more than a low quality product with a low share.

In another book *Perspectives in Experience,* the Boston Consulting Group propound the theory that costs reduce with accumulated experience. More precisely costs decline by between twenty and thirty per cent every time accumulated volume doubles. The relevance of market share in this context is that costs will decline faster for the business with the larger share as experience accumulates faster. This of course leads to greater strategic strength and/or profitability.

All of this goes to prove the necessity for accurate data on market size and market shares. Whilst the fast-moving consumer goods companies will have their Neilsen statistics readily available, data of this type are less common in companies manufacturing goods for industry and commerce. Yet it is still

* *PIMS: A Breakthrough in Strategic Planning.* Marketing Science Institute, December 1973.

equally desirable. Even crude estimates are better than no information at all.

It is obviously important to know market size and the rate at which it is growing, or declining. Market shares expressed in units and value are both vital to strategic planning (the two measurements of share can, of course, be significantly different).

Sales and margin performance

The first step in estimating future performance is naturally to audit the sales and gross margin forecast in great detail—if one exists. To be able to assess this forecast thoroughly, however, a considerable amount of supporting information is needed, principally: historical data in terms of units, sales value and percentage gross margin over a period of at least three years; actual results for the current year to date; a summary of objectives and planned actions, including pricing changes, for the year in question; projected product costs; trends in industry sales expressed as percentage changes year by year. If the historical sales figures also give performance against forecast in the years surveyed this is another useful, but not essential, fix on the accuracy of the forecast under audit.

It makes life much easier if the information needed is grouped on simple forms, logically arranged. Tables 5.1, 5.2 and 5.3 show forms which have proved very useful in this respect. The examples given are totally fictitious but they demonstrate how easy the forms are to use and how clearly they communicate essential data and trends.

To prove the point let us work through the examples and draw the obvious conclusions. Consider each form in turn.

Table 5.1 Sales and gross margin forecast

Product A. Here we see zero growth in units with a higher sales value resulting from an 11 per cent price increase or a decrease in trade discounts. Margin has risen by 6 per cent and it would

Table 5.1. Sales and gross margin forecast–78/79

COMPANY: J. Smith & Co. PRODUCT GROUP: Nuts & Bolts Division

Product	*Planned unit sales*	*Actual unit sales YTD**	*% increase on current plan*	*Av. net selling price*		*Planned sales*	*Planned gross margin*	*Gross margin %*	
				Planned	*Current actual*			*Planned %*	*Current actual %*
Product A	10 000	8000	–	2.00	1.80	20 000	10 000	50%	44%
Product B	5000	4000	4%	5.00	4.75	25 000	15 000	60%	54%
Product C	50 000	35 000	19%	3.00	3.40	150 000	100 000	67%	62%
Total	65 000	47 000	8%	3.00	3.25	195 000	125 000	64%	55%

*Unit sales period: 9 months

appear that costs have remained constant. The question which remains at this stage is whether units will stay the same following the price increase.

Product B. We have a 4 per cent increase in units, a 6.6 per cent increase in price (or a reduction in discounts), resulting in at 6 per cent increase in margin. Costs seem to have reduced by 9 per cent. The figures look reasonable.

Product C. Units are up by 19 per cent, and price reduced by 12 per cent. Margin is also increased by 5 per cent. The questions to be asked here are whether the units are possible and whether the effective price decrease is wise.

Table 5.2: Historical sales performance

Product A. We see a fast decline in unit sales in spite of holding the price. A further decline in units seems likely. Gross margin has reduced steadily which makes the forecast margin increase decidely questionable This product has a lessening importance in terms of total sales.

Product B. Units are increasing steadily which makes the forecast seem possible. Prices and margin are increasing too which also points to a conservative forecast.

Product C. The rate of unit increase is decreasing steadily. It would appear, therefore, that the forecast unit increase is unlikely in view of the price/volume relationship. Our objective should be to maximise gross margin value but the figures indicate a potential reduced margin based on forecast units and price. Given this situation it is a simple matter to project graphically the trend in units against price and margin against units. The resultant graphs clearly show that it would be profitable to maintain price and current unit volume (see Figure 5.2).

Table 5.3: Market size and company sales

Product A. Market share is decreasing steadily in a virtually

Table 5.2. Historical sales performance
— COMPANY: J. Smith & Co.
PRODUCT GROUP: Nuts & Bolts Division

Product line	*Unit sales*	*Sales value*	*Av. net selling price*	*% gross margin*	*% of product group sales*
Prior year 1975–1976					
Product A	20 000	34 000	1.7	53%	19%
Product B	4000	16 000	4.0	37%	9%
Product C	30 000	126 000	4.2	52%	72%
Total	54 000	176 000	3.3	51%	100%
Last year 1976–1977					
Product A	15 000	27 000	1.8	50%	14%
Product B	4500	19 800	4.4	45%	10%
Product C	38 000	144 400	3.8	58%	76%
Total	57 500	191 200	3.3	56%	100%
Current year (projection) 1977–1978					
Product A	10 000	15 000	1.8	44%	8%
Product B	4800	21 600	4.75	54%	12%
Product C	42 000	142 800	3.4	62%	80%
Total	56 800	179 400	3.2	60%	100%

Table 5.3. Market Size & Company Sales

COMPANY: J. Smith & Co. PRODUCT GROUP: Nuts & Bolts Division

	Last year 1976–1977			*Projection current year 1977–1978*			*1st Year plan 1978–1979*		
Product line	*Total market sales*	*Company sales*	*Market share* %	*Total market sales*	*Company sales*	*Market share* %	*Total market sales*	*Company sales*	*Market share* %
Product A	180 000	27 000	15%	170 000	15 000	9%	175 000	20 000	11%
Product B	247 500	19 800	8%	250 000	21 600	9%	250 000	25 000	10%
Product C	481 500	144 400	30%	470 000	142 800	30%	475 000	150 000	32%
Total	909 000	191 200	21%	890 000	179 400	20%	900 000	195 000	22%
% increase over previous year	+2%	+5%		(2%)	(6%)		+1%	+9%	

Figure 5.2 Product C: price/volume, cost/volume and resultant gross margin

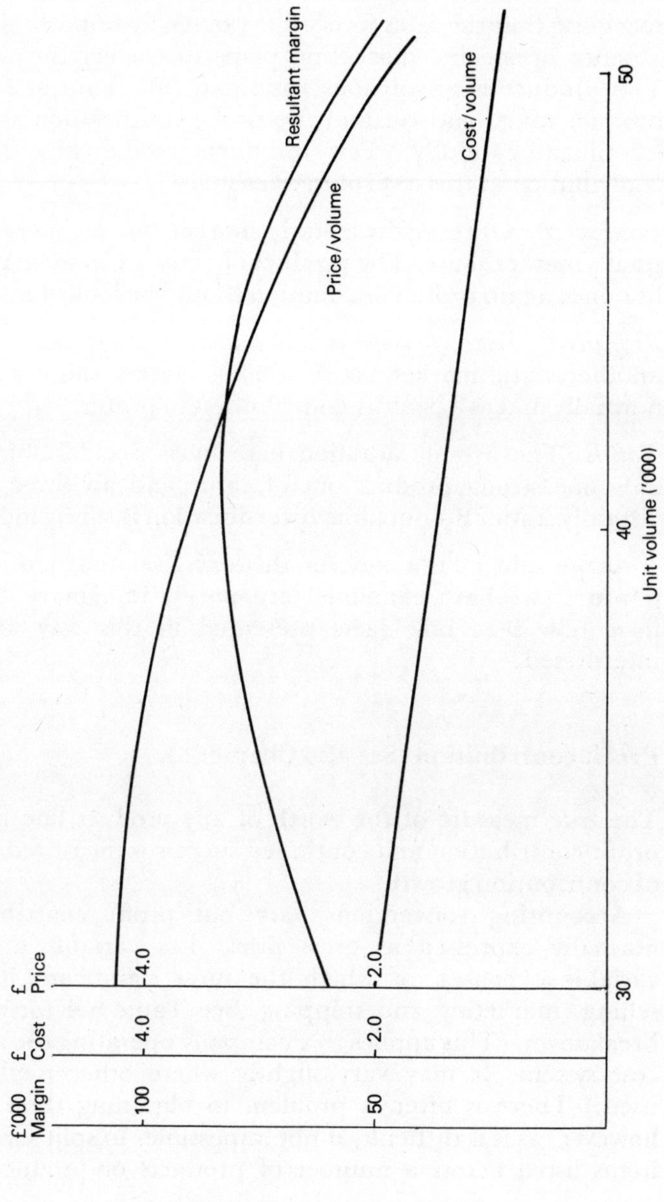

static and small market. Almost certainly now, we must recognise that the sales forecast is extremely improbable in the absence of specific marketing plans to correct the situation. The product is an obvious candidate for removal from the product range and certainly its profit contribution should be examined carefully. Few products make any form of contribution at this level of market share.

Product B. Once again a static market but an increasing, if small, market share. The product obviously has some potential but once again profit contribution should be looked at closely.

Product C. Here we have reached a static share position in yet another static market. With a 30% market share a product normally makes a healthy contribution to profits.

Totals. The overall situation here looks decidely bleak with only one strong product out of three and all three markets virtually static. Product line diversification is surely indicated.

As we said at the start of this exercise, the numbers and products we have examined are purely imaginary. But you have now seen how facts presented in this way are easily interpreted.

Profit contribution (See also Chapter 3)

The true measure of the worth of any product line lies in its profit contribution and continued success is measured in terms of contribution growth.

Accounting conventions vary but profit contribution is normally expressed as gross profit less variable and semi-variable expenses, of which the most significant items are selling, marketing and shipping. See Table 5.4 for a typical breakdown. (This applies to a company operating the standard cost system. It may vary slightly where other methods are used.) There is often a problem in obtaining these figures, however, as it is difficult, if not impossible, to split some of the items listed across a number of products or product groups

Table 5.4. Contribution analysis (£000's)

					Current Year				
Prior year	*% sales*	*Last year*	*% sales*	*Description*	*Plan*	*% sales*	*Actual*	*% sales*	
				Net sales					1
				Cost of sales (at standard)					2
				Standard margin (1–2)					3
				Total variances to standard					4
				Service repair costs					5
				Inventory provision					6
				Total cost of sales (2+4+5+6)					7
				Gross profit (3 –7)					8
				Commission					9
				Shipping costs					10
				Duties					11
				Royalties					12
				Field selling					13
				Promotion, advertising					14
				Marketing					15
				Market research					16
				Other					17
				Total variable and semi-variable expenses					18
				Contribution (8 –18)					19
				% contribution (19/1)					20

where the expenditure in question relates to more than one of them. Selling expenses, for example, usually present this problem and an arbitrary split is probably the only possible solution.

The importance of these figures is less in their absolute values than in their percentage to sales relationship, one to another, year by year and, of course, against budget in the current year. Our audit should identify trends, say, in advertising expenditure as a percentage to sales and establish reasons for this. If, of course, there is no good reason for this, or any other, trend we identify, corrective measures should be taken.

Presentation of information

We have now come to the point in our audit where we have amassed all the data necessary to arrive at broad strategic decisions. Because there is such a mass of information, however it is advisable to filter this and structure what remains in such a way that logical decisions are immediately apparent. Table 5.5 is as good as any method we have yet discovered.

The examples illustrated here are reasonably clearcut but, of course, they will not always be as straightforward. In these

Table 5.5. Possible product information display

	Product A	*Product B*	*Product C*
Sales as % of product group or company	8%	12%	80%
Market share	11%	10%	32%
Market growth	−10%	1%	−2%
Gross margin	44%	54%	62%
Margin growth	−6%	−9%	4%
Profit contribution	−5%	1%	35%

cases, product A is clearly a 'dog' product and one should endeavour to pull out of this business. At the other end of the scale, product C is a 'cash cow' and should be carefully maintained. It is with product B where the decisions become more difficult. It currently contributes little but it appears to be growing fast in a virtually static market. Clearly, further studies are required on the potential in terms of gains in market share, the cost of growth and the likely profit contribution at higher levels of market share. The only real alternative to rapid growth with this product is to get out of the business completely.

Product life cycle (PLS)

The product life cycle concept came to the fore a few years ago and in many companies is still a part of the current strategic armoury. The idea of the PLS is that every product or class of products, has a finite life and during this life follows a typical introduction/growth/maturity/decline pattern as illustrated in Figure 5.3

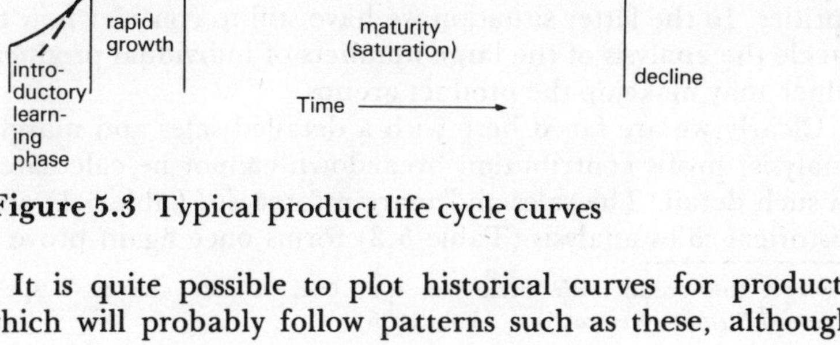

Figure 5.3 Typical product life cycle curves

It is quite possible to plot historical curves for products which will probably follow patterns such as these, although there are many exceptions. The difficulty lies in plotting curves for current products and trying to predict at which stage in the life cycle the product is positioned and what is likely to happen in the future. A recent article in the *Harvard Business Review** quotes research done into the subject of predicting future trends using the PLS concept as a basis for assumptions. After examining over one hundred product categories it was concluded that, in the vast majority of cases, application of the PLS concept was likely to do more harm than good. Perhaps the most significant statement in this article is the following:

> 'Clearly the PLS is a *dependent* variable which is determined by marketing actions; it is not an *independent* variable to which companies should adapt their marketing programmes.'

If, in the course of our marketing audit we come across PLS curves, obviously they are worth examination but always remembering that they do portray the results of past marketing actions, good or bad, and that changes in strategy can bring changes in the curves. Many products, supposedly in their maturity stages, have been given new leases of life by the adoption of new strategic ideas.

Multi-product analysis

The techniques discussed so far apply to the analysis of a limited range of individual products or, alternatively, they equally well apply to product groups considered as total entities. In the latter situation we have still to consider how to tackle the analysis of the large numbers of individual products which may make up the product groups.

Clearly we are faced here with a detailed sales and margin analysis; profit contribution breakdown cannot be calculated in such detail. The sales and margin forecast (Table 5.1) and historical sales analysis (Table 5.2) forms once again prove a

*'Forget the product life cycle concept', N.K. Dhalla and S. Yuspeh, *Harvard Business Review,* Jan. – Feb. 1976.

very useful basis for the performance of this task alongside year-to-date results; it is more essential than ever when handling large quantities of information to assemble the facts simply, logically and tidily.

Our survey has two major objectives: to weed out the weak products in the range and then to identify areas of weakness in the products which remain. The first move, therefore, is to identify the good sellers and the bad sellers, the high margin contributors and the low margin contributors. Almost certainly the eighty/twenty rule will apply more or less, so a useful exercise is to find the top twenty per cent of sales and margin generators and measure their contribution as a percentage of the total. (Quite frequently the two are not the same and if this is so it is a useful discovery in itself).

More important at this stage is to isolate the weaker products, normally in terms of total margin generation but another interesting measure is in average margin per order compared with the average normal cost of processing an order.

One's first inclination on having identified low volume, low margin or otherwise unprofitable products is to delete them from the range. Before doing so, however, certain other factors need to be considered:

(i) Are they a necessary accompaniment to other, more profitable, products in the range?
(ii) Are sales increasing or decreasing? If increasing, at what rate and how quickly will they pull out of the weak products list?
(iii) Have they received the attention they deserve? If marketing resources were deployed to support them would they generate a positive profit contribution in a reasonable length of time?
(iv) What marketing resources do they consume currently? Could these be used more profitably elsewhere?
(v) Would product deletion have any significant adverse effects on production capacity utilisation, the costs of other products or the allocation of general overhead?
(vi) What is the current inventory of the products concerned?

How long would it take to dispose of this? Many an unwary marketing man has removed a product from his range only to be asked by the manufacturing manager months later what is to be done with the inventory of finished goods, parts or packaging.

(vii) Can the average order value be improved by some means? Perhaps by introducing a minimum ordering quantity. Or how about a small order charge?

These are the more obvious questions which should influence our decisions on the products at the bottom of the range. Others may occur according to the situation. Factors such as pricing, discounts and product costs sometimes play their part, although we are talking, of course, about products making a negligible contribution to profits so it is more than likely that changes in these areas will make little difference.

With regards to the products at the other end of the scale, we should be looking for means of profit improvement, through increased unit sales, price and discount changes, variations in the mix of products sold and finally in reduced product cost.

Product cost

(i) Value added

Before going into the details of manufacturing costs of individual products, it is a very worthwhile exercise in terms of gaining a proper understanding of a company and its product groups to analyse the value added by the company in the products it sells or the services offered. How has this varied over the years? Are there any significant changes? Manufacturing costs are only one of the elements involved. A typical example of value added analysis is given in Table 5.6.

Analyses such as these are more interesting in percentage terms than in absolute figures. They give the best indication of strengths, weaknesses and trends. In this example we see a company with a very high selling and marketing expense

Table 5.6. Value added analysis—detailed breakdown

	1975/76		*1976/77*		*1977/78*	
	000s	%	*000s*	%	*000s*	%
Manufacturing						
Standard cost (less materials)	1200		1100		1250	
Variances	800		700		650	
Inventory provisions	120		150		150	
Other mfg costs	700		800		900	
Total	2820	29	2750	32	2950	32
G & A total	1200	12	1250	14	1400	15
Selling & market						
Field selling	2000		1600		1800	
Commissions	300		240		280	
Sales management	280		300		300	
Sub-total	2580	26	2140	24	2380	26
Adv. & sales prom.	1200		1000		1015	
Product management	50		60		65	
Sub-total	1250	13	1060	12	1080	12
Freight	250		200		200	
Customer service	300		350		390	
Shipping and warehouse	500		350		400	
Sub-total	1050	11	900	10	990	11
Total S & M	4880	50	4100	47	4450	48
R & D total	400	4	200	5	300	3
Other—total	400	4	200	2	100	1
Total value added	9700	100	8700	100	9200	100

obviously trying to cut it back. And rightly so. The strategic significance of this high S & M cost is that it renders the company vulnerable to attack from companies with much lower costs in this area. The other really noteworthy item in the table is the G & A cost which is steadily increasing from a level which was already high to start with. Another area of vulnerability.

(ii) Manufacturing cost

Several product costing systems are in common use and there are many variants on these. From a marketing point-of-view the system used makes little difference. What matters is the make-up of product costs and how these have changed over the years. Table 5.7, for example shows a useful breakdown for a company using a standard cost system. More detail than this is totally unnecessary.

In these days of inflation it is not unusual to see costs rising line by line. Given that one knows average labour and material cost increases for the years in question it is not too difficult to compare these against the costs detailed and find the anomalies. In the example the first items to question are packaging labour and departmental overhead (which is often a function of labour cost).

In our audit we need to examine the costs of all products in a simple way such as this, raising questions where necessary, noting problem areas and trying to arrive at solutions or institute specific corrective actions.

Whilst costs are generally regarded as the responsibility of the manufacturing department, it makes sense for Marketing to be able to go over them and raise questions such as these; costs do after all have a very significant influence on margins.

The question should also be asked of Manufacturing whether they have a regular cost reduction programme and what it is. Marketing should have a decided influence on the selection of products for value analysis/cost reduction. Usually it is essential for the two departments to collaborate on such projects. Taking packaging as the obvious example,

Table 5.7. Standard cost—product X

	1975/76	% *change*	*1976/77*	% *change*	*1977/78*	% *change*	*1978/79*	% *change*
Material cost	11.51	—	11.74	+2%	11.99	+17%	12.50	+4%
Production labour	2.57	—	1.75	(32%)	1.90	+9%	2.10	+10%
Packaging	3.21	—	3.21	—	3.40	+6%	3.60	+6%
Packaging labour	1.02	—	1.31	+28%	1.50	+14%	1.75	+17%
Tool amortisation	0.28	—	0.28		0.28	—	—	
Dept. overheads	1.55	—	2.07	+34%	2.50	+21%	2.90	+16%
Contribution cost	20.14	—	20.36	+1%	21.57	+6%	22.85	+6%
General overhead	4.33	—	4.68	+8%	5.10	+9%	5.30	+4%
Standard cost	24.47	—	25.04	+2%	26.67	+6%	28.15	+6%

Manufacturing may recommend ways of reducing costs in this area but Marketing must necessarily have the final say. Anything affecting appearance, quality or performance must obviously meet with Marketing's blessing. Selection of priorities is another subject for collaboration.

Final conclusions

We have now completed our product line audit. Perhaps we could have done more. For specific products other standards of performance will immediately suggest themselves. But here we have considered the essentials, whatever the product. Do all of this and the future will become much clearer.

Key audit points

1. Are basic facts about the products themselves properly documented? Features, advantages, benefits, interrelationships, for example.
2. Does product packaging reflect the desired company or brand image?
3. Can we economise on packaging costs without loss of quality?
4. Have all competitive products been tested and compared with our own? Are the results documented?
5. How does the competition's product positioning relate to our own? Do they have any exposure? Do we?
6. Do we know market size, our share and trends in size and share?
7. How accurate is the sales and margin forecast in the light of historical trends, market trends, market share, planned strategies? How accurate were previous forecasts?
8. Do we have a detailed breakdown of profit contribution by product line or product group? Are any significant trends apparent in the totals or any of the expense items?

9. Is the product life cycle concept used as a basis for strategic thinking? How valid are the assumptions made?
10. Which are the top twenty per cent of sales and margin generators? What percentages of the total results do they represent? Does the eighty/twenty rule apply?
11. Which are the weak margin generators?
12. Do we know the average cost of processing an order? How do average order values per product relate to this? Can we improve average order values?
13. Should we delete apparently weak products from our range? Have we considered: product interdependence; trends; resource consumption; effects on production; inventory levels?
14. Are there significant changes in the value added by any departments of the company over the last few years? Where do our strengths and weaknesses lie in this respect?
15. Do we have a breakdown of manufacturing costs per product. Are any changes in cost out of line with normal trends?
16. Do Manufacturing and Marketing liaise on cost reduction programmes? What are these programmes?

6 Pricing and discounts

'Our country has plenty of good five-cent cigars, but the trouble is they charge fifteen cents for them.'

Will Rogers

Centuries ago, when marketing really began, the only marketing mix variables were product and price. Price and volume were the key determinants of success or failure. Now, with our increased sophistication, mass distribution, national and international advertising, pricing has tended to take a back seat to its more glamorous co-workers. In many companies, pricing is a once or twice a year activity, whilst other variables such as advertising or sales force are a full-time occupation. This is not to say that pricing can, or should, occupy an equivalent amount of time but, remembering that an increase in price has an immediate and almost equivalent effect on profitability, it certainly does merit regular attention in the form of research, analysis and, possibly, adjustment.

Economists still dwell on the theories of supply and demand linked to price. At the same time they see a relationship between volume and cost. It is a simple step from here, therefore, to show the connection between the price/demand curve and profitability.

If price-setting were truly as simple as this there would be no need for marketing men, in this area at least. Unfortunately this simplistic view of pricing ignores numerous factors which have appeared since those early days of market trading. Competitive products are not identical in this day and age.

Quality varies. So does packaging. What about brand image and consumer preference? Economic theory relates only to short-term profitability. In many companies this is considered less important than profits in the long-term. How does one measure demand? What is the distributive influence on demand? Where is the influence of advertising, sales promotion and public relations? Is it really possible to measure costs in relation to increased demand with any degree of accuracy? Factors such as these prevent us from directly applying economic theory to ninety-nine per cent of products, even though the principles are always at the back of our minds.

Pricing is an art, not a science. It is a complex subject which can be made easier by the use of a logical approach: assembling all known facts and making assumptions or decisions based on these. The trouble is that decisions are often made without going to the trouble of gaining the facts.

Objectives of the audit

We must recognise from the start that we are not in the business here of fixing or recommending prices but rather in examining a pricing structure in the light of available facts.

The objectives of this study, therefore, are:

(1) To gain an understanding of all factors influencing prices and pricing decisions in the relation to the products surveyed.
(2) To examine prices and pricing policy and assess whether these are in line with overall marketing objectives.
(3) To draw general conclusions and make recommendations based on these findings.

Audit strategy

It follows from our objectives that the primary function of our pricing audit is to examine the facts: all data relevant to pricing and pricing decision-making. By asking a limited number of basic questions it is in fact possible to draw firm conclusions about the strength of a pricing policy and resultant decisions. Of course, everything should tie in very closely with overall marketing objectives. A key factor, for instance, is whether we are more interested in long-term profitability than high profits in the short term.

Assembling the facts

From experience we have found that a question-and-answer approach under a relatively small number of headings to be the best way of tackling this problem. In common with most marketing plans or surveys we start with a study of the market before proceeding to a detailed examination of company and product data.

1. The market

1.1. Market evolution

Markets, like products, go through a life cycle, largely determined by the collective marketing activities of the interested companies. As already discussed in Chapter 4, the normal life cycle has four main stages: low introductory growth; a period of rapid growth; the mature stage with little or no growth; finally the decline. Whilst one can argue about the predictability of each stage and the value of the product life cycle concept in overall marketing planning, it is very important from the point-of-view of pricing to know which stage the market has reached in its evolution, as pricing policies tend to change with each stage.

In the early introductory stages competition is either very limited, or non-existent, costs are relatively high and hence prices also are often high. In the growth stage, however, competition becomes a major consideration: how to keep them out, or how to gain or maintain share. Costs fall too as volume increases. Hence the net effect is for prices to come tumbling down. As maturity sets in, competitive stances are known, overall growth has slowed down, so prices tend to stabilise. When the market eventually declines, some competitors disappear, costs become a problem as total volume falls but prices again tend to fall in the desperate search for a higher share of what remains.

The obvious questions to be asked under this heading, therefore, are: where does the market stand in its life cycle—introduction; growth; maturity or decline. If it is in the growth stage, is there a known limit to this growth? What is the rate of growth in terms of unit sales?

1.2. Competition

How many competitors do we now have in the market? Are more likely to arrive? Are there are reasons why competition might find it hard or undesirable to enter the market? Possible reasons might be the high cost of entry, patent protection, technical difficulties, limited market size or profit potential.

1.3. Pricing sensitivity

What type of market is it in terms of pricing sensitivity? In other words, how sensitive is the consumer to variations in price for this kind of product? For many product categories, pricing is an extremely critical factor in the purchasing decision, for others less so. For example, sensitivity is high where there is a high frequency of purchase (food, confectionery, detergents fall under this heading) or where there is a low frequency of purchase alongside a high unit price (cars, washing machines, televisions, etc.). It is also high where price comparisons are readily available. But where purchases are infrequent, prices relatively low and comparisons difficult to make, price variations have much less significance. Products with a high fashion or fad appeal also fall under this heading: perfume being the obvious example here.

It is vitally important that we recognise consumer attitudes to price levels, changes and differentials. At the same time, we should not forget the probable reaction of the trade.

2. Company data

2.1. Product evolution

How long has the product been on the market? At which stage in its life cycle do we believe it stands? Or rather, at what stage is our business? Is it growing? Fast or slowly? Obviously we will have available historical and current sales figures, plus projections, both in units and value. This should give us the trend. How does this relate to the trend in the total market. If it differs, why is this? Does pricing play any part in the difference?

2.2. Pricing methods

How are prices determined? Do we have a standard procedure and has this always been the case? How was our share affected if and when we changed our method?

There are three basic methods which could be used, each with several variations: cost-plus, competitive pricing or demand pricing.

(i) The cost-plus system has three common variants: a percentage mark-up on cost; pricing to give a fixed percentage gross margin; target pricing.

Mark-up is the simplest way of pricing and is most frequently used in retail shops and the engineering and construction industries. Its advantages are that it is not dependent on the vagaries of demand and where all companies in the market use the same system, it also results in reasonably similar pricing levels. From the consumer's viewpoint, it is a fair system as prices do not usually rise with higher demand. The buyer, on the other hand, is guaranteed a fair return on his investment. Unfortunately, the disadvantages of the system by far outweigh the advantages, principally because it does not take account of the elasticity of demand and also because it is virtually impossible to determine a percentage uplift which will optimise profit.

The fixed gross margin variant suffers from similar disadvantages. it becomes useful, however, in a company selling a wide range of products, or numerous variations of a few products, where other methods would be impracticable and where it has been established what margin will be necessary to cover budgeted costs provided sales are also to budget, or above.

Target pricing goes one step beyond this even. Here a company establishes the price which would give it a desired rate of return on its total costs for an estimated fixed volume. To be able to do this accurately, the company needs also to estimate total costs across a range of volume levels up to full capacity. The major flaw in the system is that it takes no account of demand at each price level; it assumes that the specified units can actually be sold. If they are not then there are major problems.

(ii) There are also three significant variations of competitive pricing: going-rate; tender, sealed-bid or contract; pricing for market share.

Going-rate pricing is very common in major industries such as steel, oil, chemicals and amongst some food products. This is the situation where competitive prices are closely grouped together and supply, or capacity, exceeds demand. There is little point in pricing above the group, unless one is cast in the role of price leader, as demand becomes elastic, i.e. falls off, and others will not follow. Similarly, lowering price has little effect, other than to reduce profitability, as most of the others will eventually follow, leaving demand as it was. The best way of gaining share in this situation is to modify or improve the product itself, and/or the services accompanying it.

Tender, sealed-bid or contract pricing is the businessman's roulette. With a good system the odds can be reduced but it is still a very imprecise cost with no second chances for the losers. The most usual way of reducing the odds is to estimate the profits and probability (on a scale of 0 to 1.0) of obtaining the business at a range of price levels. The two multiplied together indicate the expected profit return at each price level and hence it is theoretically possible to determine the best price for the tender. The main difficulty, of course, lies in estimating the probabilities.

Pricing for market share, simply means pricing against competition, recognising, of course, that competition does not like losing share and will probably react if this happens. In considering this approach, one should also think about alternative ways of achieving the same ends: by changes in product quality, packaging or supporting services; alternatively by the use of advertising, sales promotion and public relations.

(iii) Demand pricing is the nearest to what economic theory would have us do. Ideally, if we were in possession of a price/demand curve for our product it would be possible to select the price that would generate the maximum profitability. Unfortunately, this is rarely, if ever, the case. Two forms of demand pricing are in common use, however: market 'creaming' and price discrimination.

'Creaming' or charging a premium price for a product often occurs at the introductory stage of the product life cycle. Whilst it has a great attraction in the short term, it is also very dangerous, if not handled with the utmost care. Generally it can be used where for some buyers product necessity outweighs cost considerations, where demand is relatively inelastic, where the unit costs of production and distribution for a low volume are not very much greater than for a much higher volume, and where there is little danger of attracting competition, because the barriers to entry into the market are relatively high. If creaming persists there is little doubt that at some stage one or more competitors will arrive, believing that the disadvantages of entry are less than the potential profits in the long term. When this happens, prices must necessarily fall.

Price discrimination occurs when a product is sold at more than one price dependent upon customer, time, place or marginal product difference. Discrimination by customer is infrequent—and in some countries totally illegal. It is rarely considered in a planned approach to pricing. But nevertheless, it can happen, when a particularly strong customer puts on the pressure for a lower price, for example.

Discrimination by time is much more common. Off-peak tariffs for electricity fall into this category. The airlines are past masters in the art too. The most obvious example of discrimination by place is found in the cinema or theatre, where different prices are charged for different seats. Finally, discrimination by product difference occurs when prices for slightly different versions of the same product vary more than the cost differences involved.

A change in colour, packaging or additional features can result in a different price—often a disproportionally higher price but occasionally a lower price to persuade the buyer to trade up and hence increase overall cash flow.

The major risks involved in price discrimination are clear: one can make the differentials too great and lose the most profitable segment; or one can segment the market incorrectly and lose volume, because of inadequate capacity; finally there is always the chance that one might alienate or antagonise customers paying the full price if they were not aware of the cheaper alternative.

These then are the most common pricing methods. Having identified which of them is used by the company being audited, the open question is whether this is the best method for the particular products or whether an entirely different method or an adaptation would be better suited to them.

2.3. Reaction to cost changes

Theory has it that costs, in non-inflated dollars, fall as experience, in terms of accumulated volume, increases. A strong strategic pricing approach in this situation is to let prices fall with costs. This is a sure way of maintaining, if not gaining, market share and hence ensuring that volume continues to increase rapidly resulting in further reductions in cost. In most companies however, the usual problem to be faced is one of cost increases. How to handle them with respect to prices. In our audit we should look for a sensible approach to this situation. Are prices re-examined logically, following the agreed methods, as costs increase, or is someone making fast, *ad hoc* decisions without going through the normal thinking process?

We have come across cases quite recently of prices which have not changed for years, sometimes because of sales force resistance (a very common reason), sometimes because of an unproven fear of volume losses, other times because of neglect or sheer carelessness. This sort of occurrence is most frequent in companies with a large range of products and product variations.

Making price increases often requires courage. But the surprising thing nowadays is how readily people accept such changes.

2.4. Variables related to price

When looking at pricing, there are many other related factors which should be taken into consideration. It is quite possible, for instance, to hold price but alter size or quantity to achieve the same results as a price increase. Has this been considered? We should also think about other non-price benefits that we might offer the consumer as a justification for higher prices: extra service, guarantees, special delivery arrangements, systems benefits, general terms and conditions. Each of these must be taken into account in our survey.

2.5. *Trade terms*

The weaker manufacturer frequently tries to gain shelf space by offering better terms to the trade, usually in the form of higher discounts. And in the short term this approach can succeed. In the long run, however, success depends on whether the goods sell through to the consumer and this is where our emphasis should lie.

Trade discounts are always a problem. In our audit we should endeavour to determine how our discount structure rates against that of competition and also against the norms for that type of product. Is it possible to reduce them? In the short term this is probably difficult to do, dependant on the strength of demand for our products, but reduced discounts can be planned as new products are introduced.

What else do we offer the trade? How about quantity discounts? What effect do these have on our profitability? Do we offer special terms for prompt settlement of accounts? If so, does the trade simply regard this as an additional discount or do we derive the proper benefit from them?

Do we offer the trade full marketing support in the form of: merchandising assistance; cooperative advertising programmes; assistance—financial or otherwise—with catalogue entries, sales force training and accompaniment; provision of sales leads resulting from our own advertising and promotional efforts? Whilst none of these factors are directly linked to our pricing and discount structure, they do have a definite effect on our standing in the trade and hence strengthen our position when it comes to decisions on discounts and terms. We should certainly include these influencing factors in our pricing audit.

2.6. *How do we rate against competition?*

The normal decision making sequence for a typical consumer is as follows:

What do I think of the product?
What is its price?
What do I get for the price?
How does this relate to alternatives?

It follows from this that we obviously need a detailed comparison of our prices vis-à-vis competitive products: price against price; discount against discount; quality against quality; extras against extras. The positioning of our products against competition is extremely important.

Whilst much of this information can well be presented in tabular form, a graphical representation of the key information serves to make the situation so much more simple. For instance, Figure 6.1 demonstrates clearly the relationship between price and product quality. Figure 6.2 is an interesting way of demonstrating how price relates to market share. The same format can be used for other combinations of variables, of course.

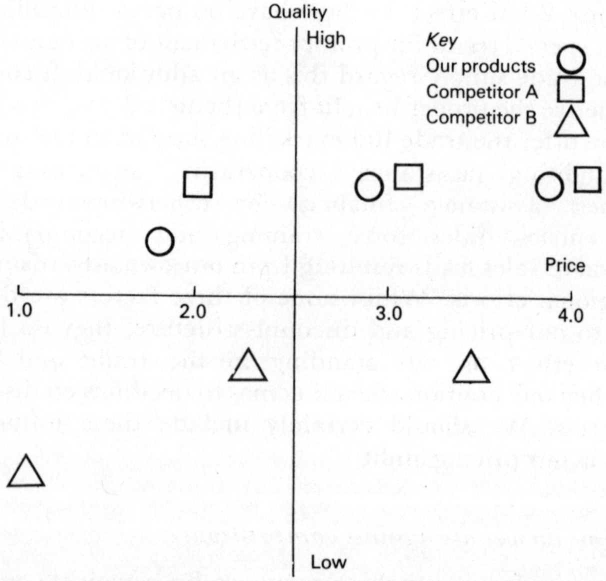

Figure 6.1 Relationship between price and product quality

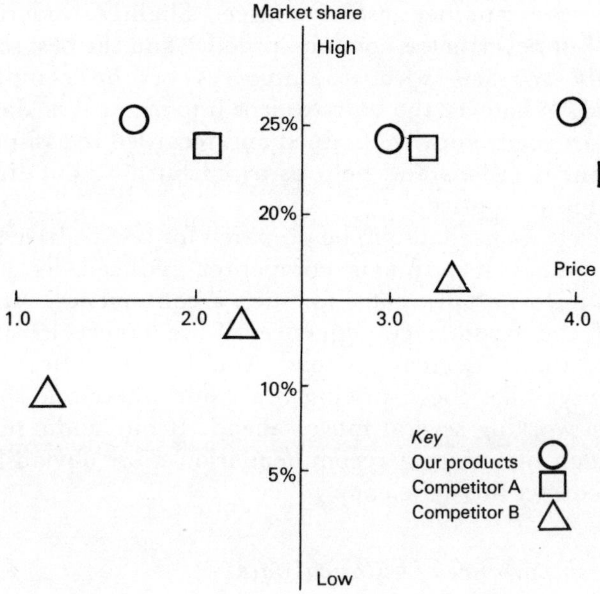

Figure 6.2 Relationship between price and market share

2.7. How does the competition fix its prices?

What do we know about competitive pricing strategies? Do they follow a similar system to ourselves or do they use other methods? Why the difference? How profitable are they? Would they welcome a general price increase?

It is, of course, very important to know, or at least predict fairly accurately, what competitors will do if we change our prices. What would they think, for example, if we increased our prices by ten per cent tomorrow? How would they react? Another obvious question here is one on price leadership: who follows whom? Or is the market so unstructured and/or uninformed that there is no real price leader?

There are many ways of obtaining such information. Historical studies reveal much of what we need to know. Salesmen's contacts with the trade and often with competitors' salesmen, are another useful source. Slightly underhand perhaps, but nevertheless common practice and the best source of all are contacts with ex-employees of the companies concerned. Whatever the sources, it is important that data of this type are methodically obtained and recorded to assist us in making our decisions and help us avoid burning our fingers when we move on price.

Conversely we need also to be prepared for competitive price changes. What if a major competitor reduced its prices tomorrow? Do we have plans for such a contingency? Are we aware of the possible consequences if we ignore it? If we matched their decrease, how would this affect our profitability? Like chess, pricing is a game where one should always be working several moves ahead. If our audit reveals lack of such planning, a recommendation must obviously be made to correct this deficiency.

2.8. The importance of historical data

Probably the most important data of all are historical statistics over at least three years showing pricing in relation to unit sales, market share, unit costs, gross margin and possibly profit contribution. Not only do we need this for our own products but as much as possible for our leading competitors'.

For convenience the information should be presented in a simple form on the lines of Table 6.1.

The figures in this table should tell us a great deal about the effects of pricing changes: how changes in price affect market share and volume; how costs change with volume; the trends in all these factors. Of course, there are other influences at work apart from price, most of which have been discussed in previous questions. The contribution percentage will tell us whether there have been any signficiant increases or decreases in expenditure which might have caused volume fluctuations.

2.9. Effects of pricing on volume and hence volume on costs

Two significant questions still remain. Do we know how elastic

Table 6.1. Comparative historical price data

Year					
RSP					
Av. net sell. price					
Unit sales					
Gross margin %					
Unit cost					
Market share					
Profit contrib. %					

the demand for our products really is—other than from the historical data given above? Perhaps we have organised pricing tests. Or perhaps we should. How does volume affect costs and the utilisation of plant capacity? In other words, if a price reduction doubles the volume sold, what effect does this have on costs and hence on profitability? (We are almost back at pure economic theory again.)

Pricing strategies and marketing objectives

One rarely comes across a true pricing objective. Most commonly these are really strategies designed to support marketing objectives. Pricing, after all, is only a means to an end, not an end in itself.

Marketing objectives, where pricing can have a definite influence, usually relate to sales revenue, profitability in terms of margin or contribution, unit volume, market penetration and gaining, or holding market share.

Pricing strategies must of course support marketing objectives and one of our main tasks in a pricing audit is to ensure that this is the case. Planned strategies can fall under one of four headings:

(i) Market penetration—generally in a price elastic market, where holding down prices will tend to increase volume, reduce costs and discourage competition.
(ii) Creaming (as described earlier) usually in an insensitive market where a natural demand exists, in support of a profitability objective.
(iii) Pricing for increased margin/contribution—also tends to be used only where the market is price insensitive.
(iv) *Status quo*—most common of all. Designed to hold margins, sales revenue, gross margin or share.

As part of our examination we should also look for contingency strategies, ready and waiting for use in emergencies. What if a major competitor decreases his prices, improves his quality compared with ours, comes out with an economy pack or some similar action? Are we ready for this? Government pricing restrictions are common occurrences nowadays. Are we ready to put through our increases before the barrier slams down or will we be pipped at the post? (for instance).

Assessment and recommendations

The answers to the data-gathering exercise, followed by an examination of objectives and strategies should have given us a very definite feeling about the pricing situation in the company and the quality of the decision making process in relation to this subject.

Undoubtedly several of the answers provided will be rather inconclusive. This is only to be expected. Based on the knowledge we have gained, though, it should be a relatively simple matter now to recommend improvements, certainly in information systems and particularly competitive intelligence. We must remember that our most important task is to ensure that methods and prices match objectives. Where this is not the case changes are obviously required.

Recommendations on pricing can never be perfect; there are too many variables involved, numerous influences to consider and usually a lack of precise information. We must never forget, for instance, that demand can change over time, costs too. Sometimes logic does not apply; it has been known, for example, for sales to increase with a higher price, probably because the uplifted price has increased consumer confidence in the product, or perhaps has given it increased snob appeal. This only emphasises the need for sound judgment.

Neither should we neglect the very important non-price variables: service, delivery, packaging configurations, terms-of-sale, minimum ordering quantities and the like. They all form part of the total pricing package. And pricing, of course, is only one of the elements in the total marketing mix. Whilst it is necessary for convenience to examine it in isolation, final decisions should also take into account possible marketing mix variations. There are always alternative strategies. Instead of increasing prices one might try holding prices and going for volume. Or alternatively planning a smaller price increase with an increase in volume. Or we might change the product configurations, giving less for the same price. It might be possible to reduce costs in some other way and thus obtain the same margin without a price increase. All we are really saying here is that all possibilities should be considered before ariving at a decision. Commonsense must prevail.

Having decided on a course of action all changes must be carefully planned. Frequently it is not possible to move directly to the ideal situation. Government legislation might be a stumbling block. We need to think about trade reactions too. Even our own sales force might give us problems.

Salesmen are notoriously conservative when it comes to price changes. We have first to sell our ideas to them.

Above all, our recommendations must offer the maximum possible benefit with the minimum of risk, remembering that any change in this area is always a risk.

International pricing

So far we have only considered pricing in one isolated country.

What is likely to change when we talk about more than one market? What is the difference, for example, between pricing decision making for the West German market and, say, the USA? Or is there a difference?

The strict answer to this question is that there is no difference, in decision making that is. The market situation and conditions may vary but the thought process and factors for consideration remain the same: market evolution, competition, market shares, costs (probably very different), methods of pricing and the rest.

In our audit, therefore, we should tackle each market in turn, asking the same questions and following the same principles. Naturally we should always work in the currency of the country in question, never in one base currency—pounds or dollars; this can give a totally misleading impression bearing in mind frequent fluctuations in exchange rates.

An increasingly common phenomenon, particularly in the past two or three years is 'bootlegging' distribution, i.e. one rogue distributor buying in a cheap market for sale in an expensive market. Totally legal and a terrible headache for many multi-national organisations. (it obviously pleases the selling country but can spell disaster for the one at the other end). The situation usually arises because of vastly different cost structures in the markets concerned resulting in a wide variation in general price levels. Just as an example, the same Volvo car in Great Britain costs considerably less than it does in Sweden where it is made. Many products cost much less in the USA than in continental Europe. In this case the differences are due to a much more competitive situation in the USA, more discounting, higher volumes, lower labour rates and social contributions.

Once into this trap it is very difficult for the manufacturer to get out without considerable losses. Often it is inevitable anyway: to price goods in the UK at Scandinavian prices, for example, would often mean zero sales; on the other hand, to price the same product in Sweden at UK prices could lead either to losses, where an operating company is concerned or to a huge loss of potential profits when it comes to direct exports.

The problem can never be completely resolved but the risks can be lessened by careful, regular international price comparisons and consideration of these possible consequences when changes are made. All we can do in our audit is to make the comparison and point out the dangers where they apply.

Key audit points

1. Is the total market: in the introductory stage, growing fast, mature or declining?
2. If it is in the growth stage, is there a known limit to this growth?
3. How many competitors do we have now? Are more likely to arrive?
4. Are there any obvious barriers to competitive entry into the market?
5. How sensitive is the market to price variations?
6. At what stage is our product in its life cycle? How does this compare with the total market?
7. Which method do we use to determine prices: cost-plus, competitive pricing; demand pricing. The method needs to be defined precisely.
8. How are cost changes handled? Is there a logical planned approach or are decisions made on an *ad hoc* basis?
9. What non-price benefits are offered? Do we make the most of these? Could they be improved?
10. How does the trade discount compare to trade norms? Are there any means, or plans, for reducing discounts?
11. What other terms do we offer the trade? How do these relate to profitability? Could they be improved?
12. Could the total support package we offer the trade be improved?
13. How do the products reviewed compare against competition in terms of: price; quality; trade discounts; new price variables offered; market share?
14. Do we know how competition fixes its prices? Do they use a different method from us? Why?

15. Where is the price leadership, if any?
16. What would be the competitive reactions if we moved our prices up or down?
17. Do we have contingency plans against a reduction in price from competition? Have we calculated the probable effects on profitability of following suit? What would happen if we ignored the change?
18. Do we have historical data for the past three or four years covering recommended selling price, average net selling price unit sales, gross margin, unit cost, market share and profit contribution?
19. Do we have any other data on the elasticity of demand for our products?
20. How are costs affected by volume? What about capacity?
21. What are the marketing objectives in which pricing is a contributory factor?
22. Define pricing strategies if they exist. Are contingency strategies prepared for possible competitive or legislative changes?
23. Do pricing strategies tie in closely with overall marketing objectives?
24. Are international prices based on conditions in the markets concerned?
25. Have we considered the dangers of 'bootlegging' from one market to another?

7 Advertising, sales promotion and public relations

'Advertising agency: eighty-five per cent confusion and fifteen per cent commission.'

F. Allen

When it comes to advertising* the principal question to be asked is whether it receives the attention it deserves in the light of the often considerable resources employed. Most probably the answer given will be 'yes', but on probing more deeply one will find that the greatest proportion of this attention is given to creative affairs and too little to the financial commitments involved. This is natural; advertising managers are rarely employed for their ability in accounting matters, nor are they usually privy to the total picture with regard to company profitability. There are exceptions, of course.

No reasonable person will deny that advertising generates tremendous waste, particularly in the sales promotion area. The problem arises in preventing the waste before it happens.

It is a frequent occurrence also to see heavy financial commitments with little documented justification and few controls imposed. A salesman's monthly expense sheet is scrutinised more thoroughly than an expenditure of ten times that amount on a piece of artwork. A thousand dollars more or less on the agency fee receives less attention than a minor increase in the standard cost of a very unimportant product,

---

* Used throughout as a generic term including sales promotion and PR.

even though the former has a much more significant effect on overall profitability.

Why are such situations more common in advertising than in other departments? Principally because advertising is more of an art than a science, where one can predict likely results but never guarantee them (except, occasionally on mail order). It is a field where ideas abound and ideas cost money. Sometimes one hits the jackpot but this is rare. It would be wrong to stifle creativity completely but the wise general manager will always keep a fairly tight rein on this area of his business.

Scope of the audit

What, then, are we looking for in our audit? Overall, we hope to find: a sensible allotment of resources—both financial and human; tight budgetary controls; clearly defined objectives; the most cost effective use of the funds available with careful planning and control in all areas. Almost certainly we shall identify areas for improvement and probably ways of reducing wastage.

Most of the information we need will already be documented in one form or another. The remainder can be obtained through informal conversations with the persons concerned. A few days out in the field, visiting retailers, distributors and users can also be very enlightening.

The budget

There is no one correct method to determine the advertising budget a company really needs. Some methods in common practice, however, are positively bad. Particularly so is the 'fixed figure' approach, i.e. a budget which bears no relation to planned sales, marketing objectives or the work to be done. It could simply be an arbitrary decision, a figure related to the previous year's budget or somehow related to competitive activity.

Where one finds budgets determined in this way one is bound also to find inefficiency and wastage (if the figure is too high). It is also an indication of weak marketing management in the organisation, often with a strong bias towards sales or production.

More sensible budgets are related to forecast sales with a cross-reference to overall company profitability. Clearly there should also be a distinct relationship between the advertising budget and the tasks to be completed, i.e. linked to marketing objectives.

Budgetary control of advertising expenditure can and should be reasonably simple. Against each job one has merely to record the budget, commitments and expenditures. Provided jobs are budgeted accurately and records kept up-to-date little should go wrong. But it frequently does.

It all starts with planning. Ideally, appropriations per job should each be calculated before the financial year begins. Failure to do this usually leads to overspending early in the year with inadequate funds for the year-end campaigns. Alternatively it can result in the cardinal sin of overspending the budget. So here is one key audit point.

Forgotten, unplanned and unexpected items constitute another danger area. Have all regular commitments been included in the budget split? Have we considered the multitude of extras that always occur? Items such as catalogue allowances, cooperative advertising commitments that one cannot escape, local exhibitions . . . it is so easy to forget them, yet they can so quickly eat up your 'reserves' (assuming reserves have been budgeted, that is — always a wise move).

Worst of all are the unexpected extras. These always seem to arrive in the last week of the year, particularly where one is dealing with a supplier with a poor accounting department. More often than not, they turn out to be additional or delayed changes from secondary suppliers such as plate-makers or typographers.

This indicates another area for scrutiny: the detail included in, and accuracy of, budget appropriations per item.

The final check on budgetary control should of course be on

bookkeeping procedures. Do we have an accurate fix on the current position daily, or weekly? Are all commitments booked, i.e. no little surprises to come later on? No advertising manager likes to end the year with unspent budget. If he thinks this will be the case he will tend to take corrective action—more spending. Hence the importance of accuracy in the current balance.

Objectives

Advertising objectives should obviously relate to overall marketing objectives. We should have objectives for above-the-line advertising, sales promotion and public relations, for every campaign, every exhibition, each piece of literature and, in fact, every significant item of expenditure. At least this would be the logical approach to spending large sums of money. Being realistic however, it is highly unlikely that such a situation exists in more than a handful of companies although it is reasonable to expect to see good campaign objectives at the very last.

What is a good objective? For obvious reasons most advertising objectives are defined merely in qualitative terms. Wherever possible, though, quantifiable targets should be included. Ideally, for instance, the effectiveness of mass media advertising should be measured by market research. If, for one reason or another, this is impossible, then at least an attempt should be made to quantify the coverage of the target audience that has been acheived.

In our audit, therefore apart form recognising a lack of objectives we should also identify bad objectives and recommend improvements. 'Motherhood and flag' objectives are very common in this field, e.g. 'To further increase brand awareness'; 'To announce our new . . .'. These should be eliminated and replaced by practical, measurable alternatives.

Creative strategy

Two lessons to be learned from many famous brands in the consumer market are the importance of accurate market positioning and continuity of advertising theme. Products advertised in an inconsistent, haphazard manner lose out on the added values that can be obtained in this way.

For each product, product line, service or system we can expect to see an established creative strategy. This should include an accurate definition of target audience and a precise summary of the message to be conveyed.

The target audience to be reached should be covered in as much detail as possible: age, sex, social grades, special interests, etc. In selling to industry or commerce the buying chain can be quite long but one must endeavour to cover everyone of influence in the purchasing decision.

The message should be simple and memorable. It may be a summary of the most important product features and benefits. Better still would be a creative platform defined in a way similar to J. Walter Thompson's T-plan approach (Figure 7.1).

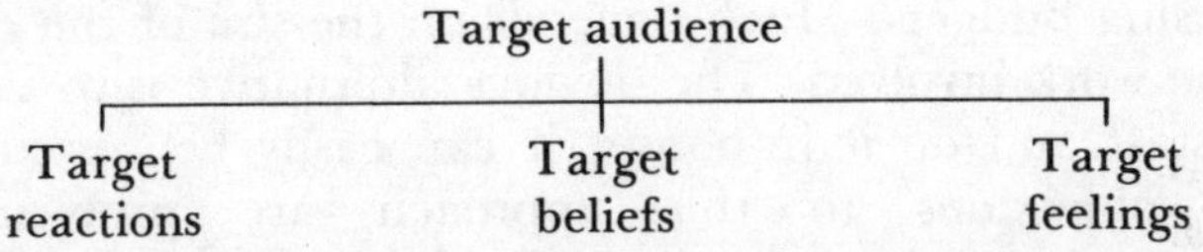

Figure 7.1 The J. Walter Thompson T-plan approach

Basically the idea here is that we are not really interested in the material itself but what emerges: what people immediately notice in the brand (target reactions); what they should believe about a brand (target beliefs) and what they should feel towards the brand (target feelings) as a result of product design, creative and media strategies.

Many other systems exist. The most important thing to check is that a creative strategy is established and that it is used as the basis for all material relating to that product inlcuding advertising, packaging and point-of-sale material. Where possible, it should also have an influence in the design of the product itself.

Millions of pounds a year are wasted on advertising that is badly briefed, ill conceived and often on an *ad hoc* basis with no continuity of creative approach. The cost is more than it appears. What these advertisers are throwing away are the opportunities to create strong brand identities for their products. You would not find Procter and Gamble doing this. The strength of our company, Dymo, in the face of a multitude of competitors, lies for a large part in its brand image.

The advertising agency

The three main points to cover when examining an agency/client relationship are:

Whether the agency is truly needed.
Whether the agency gives value for money.
Whether the client handles the relationship efficiently.

Why use an advertising agency? Is it really necessary? They certainly account for a major item of expense in many advertising budgets. Much depends on the size of the budget and the work involved. The obvious alternative is to take on more staff and do it in-house. It can easily be costed. The major objections to this approach are problems in administration, in recruiting people of sufficient calibre and in keeping them fully employed. There may also be a tendency for internal staff to become introverted with respect to the products they handle. If media advertising is involved, recoupment of commissions could prove problematic—the full amount anyway. But it is still worth re-examination.

Is it possible to measure whether an agency gives value for money? Their output depends to a certain extent on the client himself. Having once agreed an annual fee it is the responsibility of the advertising manager to extract the maximum value for the money he is paying. Quality of work and output can of course be examined. Provided this is in line with a clearly defined creative strategy, further judgment is purely subjective.

An agency is only as good as the people working on the account. It is worth spending some time, therefore, with the agency team. Not only does it enable one to assess the calibre of the people concerned, the services they provide and their business acumen, but one also learns much about their client and the way he conducts his business.

An examination of agency personnel leads naturally to the final check: how well the agency is handled. More and more agency fees are calculated on the time involved in handling a client's business. If the client wastes time by coming to a briefing meeting badly prepared or by frequently changing his mind after the meeting, the wasted time will surely be reflected in his fee next year.

The key to success here surely lies in a complete brief supported by a previously established creative strategy. A good agency brief contains the maximum amount of useful and relevant information. It could include background material such as relevant market data, historical sales figures, competitive analyses, trends in sales, research findings, market shares, consumer attitudes, increase usage preferences. Then there are product features and benefits, competitive advertising, related marketing strategies, media requirements, and so on. Finally the budget for the job. No matter what the job, the effort expended in producing a proper brief will save time, money and effort thereafter.

Procedures for progressing and approving agency work should be clearly established. Every job should have a budget coupled to an agency estimate and a progress schedule. All decisions are normally documented in the agency call report. In common with most other disciplines, advertising works best when as much as possible is reduced to a routine.

Media advertising

When advertising is being created it is quite common for media planning to take a back seat to the creative department.

This is dangerous. Even for a well-established product which has, for example, been using television as a medium for years, a time could arise when other media become a more logical choice. And, whatever the choice, the advertisements must clearly be geared to the media selected.

Prime consideration is always given, or should be, to obtaining the best coverage of the target audience at the most economical cost.

Rates change however. Coverage rises and falls. Sometimes impact is almost more important than both cost and coverage; after all, one of the main requirements of advertising is to create attention.

There is no reason, for instance, why the smaller industrial or commercial advertiser should feel himself to be confined to the trade and technical press. Several years ago, Dymo was planning to launch a pricing system for use mainly in supermarkets, independent grocers, chemists and gift shops in the London area. The obvious media selection was to use the well-known trade magazines covering these categories. The problem, however, was that to make any significant impact in, say, the *Grocer,* one would need to book a heavy series of large spaces in full colour and even then there would be a tremendous waste circulation. In the end television was selected as it was found we could obtain a fifty per cent rate reduction as a new advertiser, gain the best possible coverage of our target audience and with enormous impact. Results bore this out.

Creativity in media selection is just as important as in words and pictures. In evaluating media advertising performance this should always be considered. Media selection in relation to target audience must appear within the objectives.

For the big advertiser media advertising objectives are not too difficult to define, as research data can probably be obtained or afforded to measure results. This is rarely the case with the smaller advertiser. Necessarily it will be more of a hit and miss affair at this level, as he cannot afford market research nor to pre-test his material in any really effective way. All that one can expect is careful media analysis to give the best possible coverage of target audience plus a creative approach in line with the agreed strategy for that product.

Research carried out by trade and technical magazines over the past few years has revealed that it requires at least six regular insertions of an advertisement in any magazine to obtain worthwhile reading and noting results amongst that magazine's readership. Using less than this number of insertions, therefore, becomes a very contentious issue.

At this bottom end of the scale production costs become an even more significant factor. It can happen that artwork and mechanical costs, for one advertisement are higher than the price of several insertions. This must be allowed for in calculations on the cost of reaching the target audience. In fact, the wisdom of advertising at all under these circumstances becomes questionable.

What then should our audit reveal under this heading? First, objectives as well defined as possible. Secondly careful consideration given to all forms of media, resulting in a media plan which gives impact plus the best possible coverage of target audience at the lowest possible cost. Finally, advertisements suited to the media selected which conform to the established creative strategy for all material. A subjective assessment of quality is of course another possibility.

Direct mail

The golden rule for using direct mail is that if your audience can be identified with a reasonable degree of accuracy and if it is not too extensive, this is the medium for you. Whilst in terms of cost per thousand it is much more expensive than other forms of advertising, in terms of cost per thousand worthwhile readers it can be much more effective.

In common with all other types of advertising or promotion, however, it must start with objectives. And the most important of these should be to state whether the mailing is intended primarily to produce sales leads or whether it is intended merely to inform. So many mailings fall between these stools and the senders think they have failed. If you tell the full story in your mailpiece the recipient makes his decision on-the-spot and if the decision is negative you will hear no more.

A mailing, however clever, cannot reason or counter objections so it is usually wise to leave this to your salesmen. In the majority of cases, therefore, it would seem reasonable to produce mailings which are just sufficient to whet the appetite of the reader and lead him to apply for further information. The offer of a free gift in addition to the additional information nearly always helps to produce a much increased response rate.

Wastage therefore, is one of the things to look for in direct mail—wastage caused by sending out too much information. If, of course, there is no sales force to follow up leads, or if the operation is intended to generate orders by mail then the above comments do not necessarily apply.

But the biggest single wastage factor in direct mail is often in the lists that are used. Just as it is extremely important to select advertising media with real care, so it is equally necessary to pick and vet the right mailing lists. Ideally every company should have its own list and certainly every advertising department should aim at building them up. Names and addresses are worth money and should be treated with respect.

Very often, however, one is obliged to use a mailing house. There are many of them and most can offer a wide range of lists from bee-keepers to zoologists. All one can say here is that it pays to be extremely careful. Their lists, their sources and frequency of up-dating should all be checked before use.

Many an unwary advertising manager has spent a fortune on creativity and print only to pour it immediately down the drain by not discovering that the list he was using was ten years out of date.

The usual response rate to direct mail campaigns is between two and five per cent. Given response-orientated objectives at the conceptual stage, however, there is no reason why this should not be increased to ten per cent or more.

The true measurement of direct mail effectiveness is in cost per reply, or even better in cost per order if a system is established to make this calculation. A typical evaluation form is shown in Figure 7.2.

Direct mail cost effectiveness								
Mailing description	No. mailed	No. returns	% response	Prod. + mailing costs	No. orders resulting	Av. cost order	Total order value	Av. value/ order

Figure 7.2 Mail order evaluation form

To complete the information in this form, which incidentally can also be used to evaluate the cost-effectiveness of other types of advertising, feedback from the field should be established. A very simple three or four part form layout which can be used to follow up on all types of sales leads is shown in Figure 7.3.

One copy goes to the salesman, one held by sales management, the third is only used where the lead is passed to distribution and a control copy is held in the advertising department. A simple system, but very practical.

Exhibitions

Exhibitions are expensive. They can also prove to be the most wasteful of all promotional options, particularly the big national and international shows at home and overseas.

Whether or not a company should participate in an exhibition depends entirely on circumstances prevailing. But it is a question worth asking. Looked at logically, the only really good reason for using any promotional medium is that it offers greater cost-effectiveness in reaching one's target audience than other media. How many of us are totally logical, though? And very often external pressures, in the form of trade associations or managing directors who feel that we ought to be there because the others are, force us to operate against our better judgment. Our marketing audit, however, should examine the pros and cons for each commitment coldly and analytically, ignoring these external influences. After all, the money involved is often considerable.

Given that participation in an exhibition is necessary how does the company derive the maximum benefit from it at minimum cost? Budgets for space, shell scheme, design, stand construction and services can be pretty accurately fixed by allowing an average cost per square foot or square metre. Currently (1977-8) £100-150 per square metre can be used as a basis for calculations in the UK; overseas exhibitions will normally work out more expensive. As in any other form of buying, costs can be kept down by putting the job out to quote for both design and construction. Design costs can be reduced by incorporating reusable display units, possibly even a completely reusable stand if the economics work out right. Construction costs mount with complexity, so the design should be simple without frills. Very often money can be saved simply by using a different material or making a rounded corner square. Evidence of activities such as these indicate a well-run cost-conscious department.

Having a beautiful stand at a reasonable price is only half the battle won. It must be made to work for you. Once again objectives should be established and someone, usually appointed as stand manager, should be made accountable for achieving them. What kind of objectives? The most obvious are orders taken, worthwhile enquiries registered, interviews conducted per day. To make it really work, strategies are needed to attract people on to the stand. Invitations should be sent out in volume, inducements offered and salesmen appointed to stop passers-by and pull them aboard.

A worthwhile exercise is to visit the stand unannounced and anonymous, or get someone else to do it if you are likely to be

IMPORTANT

SALES LEAD

Source of enquiry:

Name of contact:

Position/title:

Company address:

Tel.:

Interested in:

Requests: Salesman's visit☐ Literature☐

Sample☐ Prices☐

Enquiry passed to: Salesman. . . . .

Distributor. . . . .

Date issued:

Follow-up date:

Results:

Order taken: YES/NO

Order value:

Details:

Figure 7.3 Suggested form for sales leads follow-up

recognised, and see the treatment you receive from stand staff. It is no good spending a small fortune on a stand if the salesmen working there just stand around smoking and talking to their pals. This is still a frequent sight at many exhibitions.

We have all seen the literature-gatherers who frequent most exhibitions, and trade shows. Most of what they take is money down the drain. The obvious solution is to produce a cheap exhibition give-away that can be handed out to everyone attending the show. Expensive literature should be saved for sending on to those genuinely interested after the show. That way too there is a much better chance of their reading the material, as most people take away so much on the day that they end up with a sort of information constipation.

Attention to all these final details indicates a good all-round management approach with a sense of responsibility exceeding what is normally expected.

The main criticism of large-scale exhibitions is that the visitor is bombarded with too much information in too short a time. Hence the increased interest in local shows, break-aways from the main event, one-company shows and in-plant seminars. The significant factor relevant to each of these is that preparation and organisation must be even better than for a stand at a big show. Given this, they often do more for the company than the big show could ever do. Check whether this alternative has been considered.

Point-of-sale

From one area of potential waste to another. You have only to look in the backyard of any grocer, chemist or hardware shop to discover the tremendous misuse of point-of-sale display material. Better still, look in the garage of almost any salesman and you will find material that never even reached the point-of-sale.

What causes this? There are four probable reasons: the material is not right for the job; too much is produced; the allocation per sales territory is wrong; merchandising controls are weak.

As part of the audit, all current material should be reviewed in the light of whether it conforms to the standard creative strategy, the objectives per item and whether it has been tested or researched before production. Salesmen's and trade reaction to the material should also be ascertained through field visits.

The basis for the quantities produced also needs to be established. Do they relate to usage potential at distribution or are they merely based on a set quantity per salesman or, even worse, someone's rough estimate? What checks have been conducted on the usage of previous, similar items? In the same way, one should determine whether or not the quantities allocated per salesman are realistic.

Merchandising controls generally fall within the responsibilities of sales management. It would be reasonable however, to expect to see merchandising summary sheets in the advertising department detailing what has been placed where. Without this sort of information it must be virtually impossible to determine the success or otherwise of material that has been produced.

Literature

There are four basic kinds of literature: sales promotional material; technical specifications; instruction books and price lists. Where most people go wrong is by trying to combine two or more of these. Or rather, it is not so much wrong as wasteful.

Technical specifications and instruction books should be simply written, easy to follow and neat. There is no need for extra colour except, perhaps, to clarify a point. Price lists too should be merely informative. They are not there to do a selling job. This is the role of sales promotional leaflets and brochures which, in turn, should concentrate on the main selling features and benefits of the products in question, using every possible technique to convert the reader. If price is a main selling feature then it should be included—always remembering that the brochure will be rendered obsolete when the price changes. If the equipment is simple to operate, it should be demonstrated. But under no circumstances should literature degenerate into being half promotional, half specification, as the chances are that it will achieve success in neither area. At the very best it will do the job, but at double the cost.

Quality of literature, as in all promotional material, is important. If it bears your company or brand name then it should be good.

But quality is not synonymous with colour. A black and white publication, well designed, can often look just as smart as one in four colours, sometimes better. Colour can only be truly justified where it is needed to enhance the message.

The same reasoning on print volume applies to literature as it does to display material. When too much is produced it gets wasted. Literature should be very carefully rationed out to the sales force. It should not be made easy for a salesman to leave literature where he should have taken an order.

Cooperative promotions

Wherever possible, expenditures under this heading should be geared to sales results and should be carefully planned in advance, taking advertising, merchandising, special offers and stock levels into consideration. It is most important to check that *all* forthcoming promotions are considered.

This is probably the easiest budget to overrun because of pressures applied by the trade on salesmen, and by the sales department on the advertising department. Every company dealing with the retail trade must have received letters requesting advertising support in a newspaper feature on the opening of a new store, or some similar event. Pure blackmail. If one is obliged to go along with it then every effort should be made to make it pay. A one-off congratulatory ad does no-one any good, least of all the retailer. Every advertisement department worth its salt should carry a range of stock advertisements to suit this and other applications, all with a hard product sell in them. Why not a special 'new premises' offer as standard?

Public relations

The term 'public relations' covers a multitude of sins. It includes relations with all the 'publics' of an organisation: staff, local community, government, the financial institutions, trade associations, suppliers but above all with customers and potential customers—the target audience as defined in advertising terminology. As we are concerned here with marketing performance we shall restrict ourselves to an examination of activities in this area only.

In this respect alone PR becomes another weapon in the marketing armoury alongside advertising and sales promotion. Like these two it should link in closely with overall marketing, product and campaign objectives. PR objectives should principally aim at gaining maximum favourable coverage for the company and its products in media covering the same target audience, and at minimum cost. Wherever possible objectives should be quantifiable. A quick look through the press cutting book gives one a clear idea on achievements to date. Column inches are not everything admittedly but absence thereof gives a clear warning that all is not well.

Anyone with an ounce of creativity in his blood is a budding PR expert, even more so than an advertising genius usually. It all looks so easy. As far as product publicity in trade and technical journals is concerned it probably is. A few simple principles of writing to follow, a copy of *British Rate and Data* or one of the press guides and there you are. The trouble, as many industrial editors will confirm, is that few know the simple principles or, for that matter, have a reasonable command of their own language. Consumer PR generally requires a much higher standard of literacy and it is almost essential to have established contacts with the relevant editors, so it is no place for the dabbler or the dilettante.

This then is the basic argument in favour of employing a PR consultant (who will probably claim a few more skills as well). Whether or not one should employ such a person or company is very much an area of judgment, although availability of time and funds also enters into consideration.

How much should one pay in fee? Another grey area. Many consultants, it is said, use the eye-blink test on prospective clients: 'That'll be £5000 a year, sir' (client does not flinch) . . . 'plus the cost of freelance writers' (no change) . . . 'plus expenses' . . .and so on until client blinks. Probably an exaggeration but there is certainly an element of chance in the final fee agreed. All one can do is estimate the probable work load, put a reasonable value on it and negotiate down to this level. This is the only way to assess the fee for the purpose of our marketing audit too. A word of caution: most consultants charge all out-of-pocket expenses, including telephone, stationery, printing and entertaining as extras outside the fee.

As with advertising agents, the role of the advertising manager, once a fee is agreed, is to obtain the maximum value for his money. He must sit on their tail. This is extremely important in handling PR as there is a marked tendency for performance to fall off after the first flush of enthusiasm and when the easiest stories are used up. Because of this it is vital that a plan and programme is drawn up and controlled for at least a full year.

The great merit of PR is that it is inexpensive compared with other means of communicating with the consumer. This statement should be qualified somewhat by saying that it is only inexpensive when it is handled efficiently and it produces results. It is also true to say that the claim only applies to the press relations (through press releases) side of the business. The 'events' side can work out very costly.

When properly thought through and sensibly organised, events such as press conferences, plant tours and seminars usually run smoothly and are very effective. Where one frequently runs into trouble, cost and often waste, is with the speculative consumer PR events, those stage-managed affairs which hope to attract press and TV coverage through novelty, scale, topicality, human interest and the like. So much can go wrong on these affairs: it only needs a major news story to break, or a competing event to be staged, at the same time and you are lost.

Advertising department staff

Having gone through virtually every aspect of the work of the department, its planning and organisation, it is fairly easy to draw conclusions about the quality of the staff involved and their competence. Before doing this, however, one should check whether they are all provided with good, workable job specifications, set personal objectives, controlled and evaluated regularly in a businesslike manner. It is all too easy to form judgments without really considering all the facts.

Conclusion

We have briefly covered all major aspects of the advertising department. The coverage is far from all-embracing but it does set clear guidelines for a general approach. Perhaps the most significant factors to look for are: well defined objectives for all major activities and items of expenditure; sensible planning at every step; tight controls wherever possible; and last, but certainly not least, a high standard of creativity across all items.

Key audit points

Budget

1. Does the budget relate to forecast sales and/or marketing objectives?
2. Are appropriations per job calculated before the year

begins?
3. Are all possible commitments considered?
4. Is there a contingency fund for unexpected, unplanned items?
5. Are financial records up-to-date?

Objectives

1. Do we have objectives for advertising, sales promotion and public relations?
2. Do we have campaign objectives and objectives for each major item of expenditure?
3. Are objectives practical and measurable?

Creative strategy

1. Is there an established creative strategy per product, product line or service?
2. Is the target audience specified in detail?
3. Is the message to be conveyed simple, clear and memorable?

Advertising agency

1. Is an agency really necessary?
2. Does it provide value for money?
3. Is the agency handled properly?
4. Are the agency team handling the account of a generally high standard?
5. Are advertising briefs well written, detailed and precise?
6. Are all jobs properly budgetted, estimated, planned and scheduled?

Media advertising

1. Are all possible media considered and reconsidered each year?
2. Does each media campaign have quantifiable objectives?

3. Is there a sensible insertion frequency?
4. Are production costs realistic in relation to media expenditure?
5. Does the advertising follow closely the established creative strategy?

Direct mail

1. Do all mailings conform to the basic creative strategy?
2. Does each campaign have quantifiable objectives?
3. Do the mailing pieces match the objectives?
4. Do the mailing say too much?
5. Are lists used checked for accuracy and currency?
6. Are company mailing lists being developed?
7. What response rate is planned? And achieved?
8. Do we calculate the resultant cost per sale?

Exhibitions

1. Does the stand design conform to the basic creative strategy?
2. Should we really attend the exhibitions scheduled? Are they the most cost effective way of reaching our target audience?
3. Are all cost reduction techniques employed in exhibition production?
4. Is the operation of each stand guided by set objectives?
5. Is literature wasted?
6. Have private company exhibitions been considered as an alternative?

Point-of-sale

1. Does all material produced conform to the basic creative strategy?
2. Is material regularly checked against market needs?
3. How are production quantities per item calculated?
4. How are quantities per sales territory calculated?

5. Does the advertising department have any measure of the success or otherwise, of the material it produces?

Literature

1. Does all literature conform to the basic creative strategy?
2. Does literature produced fit well into one of the four main groupings?
3. Is there duplication of information within the literature?
4. Are all colours necessary?
5. How are production quantities calculated?
6. Is the distribution and use of literature carefully controlled?

Cooperative promotions

1. Does all cooperative promotional material line up with the basic creative strategy?
2. Is most of the expenditure under this heading preplanned?
3. Are most promotions geared to sales targets for the accounts concerned?
4. Does the department carry a range of stock advertisements for this purpose? Do they sell?

Public relations

1. Are there set quantifiable objectives for public relations? Do these tie in with strategic marketing objectives?
2. Does the press cuttings book indicate success to date?
3. Does the PR consultancy fee relate to the work to be done?
4. Is there an annual plan and programme for PR? Is it under control?
5. Are PR events properly planned and managed?

Staff

1. To whom do they report? How?
2. Do they have job specifications detailing responsibilities and accountabilities?
3. Do they have personal work programmes and objectives? Are they evaluated against these?

8 Distribution, including the sales force

'It is well-known what a middleman is: he is a man who bamboozles one party and plunders the others.'

Benjamin Disraeli

In its widest marketing concept distribution can be described as the methods used to transport, store and deliver goods to the ultimate product or service user. It includes the resources allocated to performing this largely logistic function, which in most cases include the sales force. In this chapter we are therefore looking at the logistics of physical distribution and the sales force elements of this important part of the marketing mix.

Distribution remains important, not just because of its effect on every other marketing activity, but also because of the cost of the pure logistics of the physical distribution. In many consumer durable companies the cost of storage, shipping and freight equals, if not exceeds, the general and administrative costs of the company. This cost escalation has resulted in many companies re-evaluating the approach to distribution. The distribution alternatives can largely be grouped as follows:

Manufacturer—user (direct).
Manufacturer—distributer—user.
Manufacturer—retailer—user.
Manufacturer—wholesaler—retailer—user.

For ease of understanding, the last three alternatives can be grouped together as they all involve the use of channels of distribution.

Whilst the channels, their organisation and influence may change from product category to product category and from country to country, they can, from an audit viewpoint, be grouped together and as such treated separately from direct distribution.

Starting the audit of distribution in a company is often the most difficult part of the whole marketing audit. This is even more so if you are auditing a market or country with which you are not totally familiar. Our first involvement in the USA produced such a situation for us. Terminology was different, the structure and organisation of the channels was different from anything in Europe, the logistics of moving goods across the geography was of a dimension not found in any European country.

The traditional methods of channel analysis whilst helpful, did not provide us with the sufficient in-depth understanding we required. Perhaps what was really happening was that our historical, intuitive knowledge of distribution had little or no relevance to the particular problems we faced. We therefore evolved a slightly different technique in auditing distribution, which subsequently we have found to be applicable to many varied situations and countries.

With any subject matter to be analysed one has to have a reasonable understanding of the subject background. Whilst our objective here is not to teach the fundamentals of distribution systems, we believe it is worthwhile to go through a few basic elements in order fully to appreciate the audit points which subsequently follow.

We have seen that the methods or channels of distribution can be grouped into two distinct categories:

Direct to user.
Via middleman to user.

The advantages of direct distribution are that the manufacturer directly controls his product or service all the way through to the ultimate user. Middlemen become necessary because of the:

Cost of direct distribution.
Need to limit investment.
Need to add specialist know-how and expertise.
Contact requirements with large number of customers who are geographically scattered.
Customer service/delivery requirements.

These requirements lead most manufacturers to obtain the available middleman to handle the products. More often, this use of channels involves several different approaches which are determined by market, market segments, geography, urban rural requirements etc. This diverse use of channels tends to evolve, as the manufacturer grows, rather than result from a conscious decision to design a channel system. However, the effective use of the right distribution channels still remains the result of:

Determining the channel objectives and constraints.
Identifying feasible channel alternatives.
Evaluating and selecting the channel combinations to be used.
Analysing and relating company costs to each activity within total distribution policy.

Whilst these criteria are directly related to designing a channel system from scratch, they can still be effective criteria for measuring the effectiveness of a system which has evolved over the years.

The analysis of costs normally include three separate categories:

Shipping department, storage and freight costs.
Marketing service costs.
Sales force costs.

Sales force costs are included here because if the company is using distribution channels, the real cost of keeping the sales force active is almost totally related to the work it does at distribution level.

If one looks at total distribution costs, including the sales force, it soon becomes obvious that this represents a huge cost to most companies. In terms of 'value added' it often is the largest single economic activity of the company. As such, an effective audit can present tremendous opportunities to increase profitability; yet because many companies' marketing approach involves complicated distribution channel strategies, it presents unique problems for the marketing auditor. There are the obvious classical marketing methods of evaluating distribution (and these we will cover) but it seems to us they fail to provide the overall dimension of the situation and very often fall short in directly relating the real cost of a particular distribution strategy. A full understanding of the overall dimension of distribution seems therefore to be the most logical starting point. From this understanding we can then move through the more classical marketing analysis techniques used to evaluate distribution.

Understanding distribution

The understanding must encompass all the marketing functions involved in matching the supply to the market demand.

Sales force —	Contact	— Searching for buyers and sellers
	Merchandising	— Presenting and fitting goods to market demand requirements
	Selling	— Ensuring adequate supply for the demand
Advertising and promotion	— Influencing both buyers and sellers to maintain a positive attitude towards products	
Logistics	— The physical aspect of transportation and storage	

However because the different channels require different 'amounts' of the above range of services, our first steps must be to understand and quantify:

The service we supply to which categories of channel.
The costs of those services.

In most situations we have come across, companies do not analyse distribution from this aspect. They quantify and analyse the classification of channel being used—chain supermarkets, independent supermarkets, independent retailers, etc. Defining the channels in this manner is not difficult, but it does involve detailed discussions with both marketing and sales managers to obtain the knowledge of what the channels really require in terms of service, as opposed to what staff managers think they need. The example shown in Table 8.1 is from a manufacturer of stationery supplies products. The target groups range from private consumer to professional users in commerce and industry. Because of this wide spectrum of demand their utilisation of distribution channels varied from the retail store to direct suppliers to large users. The category definitions were based on detailed discussions with the marketing and sales management. Despite the complete variety of channels being used we managed to summarise them under these five categories.

Table 8.1. Channel category definitions

Category A

Limited service retailers
'Retail chains or groups where we call on the head office or regional office to conduct our business. We do not call on, service or deliver to, any of the specific outlets of that chain or group.'

Category B

Full service retailers
Independent retailers, groups or chains, cash and carry etc., where we call on, service and deliver to the specific outlets. In addition to the specific outlet calls we may also make head office calls as well.

Category C

Wholesalers—buying rings

Traditional wholesalers and their branches who resell to medium to small retailers. We provide a total service to wholesalers of merchandising, sales training, campaign planning, all of which is utilised/passed on to the retailer.

Included in this category are buying rings, who perform the same function as the wholesaler, but may or may not physically stock products.

Category D

Distributors

Specialised retailers who sell primarily to professional users via their own sales force, catalogues, direct mail, telephone, etc.

Category E

End-users

Large end-users who because of their size, importance and volume requirements are supplied direct from the manufacturer.

Our next step was to detail the service required by each category, the detail to be both quantified and summarised under the three main service headings: sales, advertising and logistics.

Tables 8.2 and 8.3 summarise the services provided to each category and details the cost of those services. The costs have been allocated both in real money terms and in terms of the percentage value added they represent (of the total company

Table 8.2. Category service requirements

	Selling & service	*Advertising & sales promotion*	*Logistics*
CATEGORY A LIMITED SERVICE RETAILERS	Monthly calls Salesmen with involvement of Regional & National Sales Manager Support promotions	Media Co-op advertising PR No advertising for private label	Monthly orders Delivery to one point or limited number of points Broad geographic spread

	Selling & service	*Advertising & sales promotion*	*Logistics*
CATEGORY B FULL SERVICE RETAILERS	Regular calls either 4 or 8 weekly Instore merchandising Sales Manager sometimes involved Support promotions Staff training	Media Coop advertising PR POS material	Medium to small orders Regular shipments Broad geographic spread
CATEGORY C WHOLESALERS	Monthly calls Head office and branches Support promotions Staff training	Trade media Coop advertising PR POS material Literature	Medium to large orders Regular shipments Controlled geographic spread
CATEGORY D PROFESSIONAL DISTRIBUTORS	Regular calls, weekly & upwards Sales training including field accompaniment Organised specific sales promotions Support national sales promotion	Vertical media Direct mail PR Literature Sales promotion Limited POS	Medium to large orders Regular shipments Broad geographic spread
CATEGORY E DIRECT TO END USERS	Regular calls	Limited literature	Small to medium orders Bids once a year Orders 1–6 times a year Controlled geographic spread

Table 8.3. Distribution cost and revenue analysis

		Turnover		*Sales & service cost*		*Advertising & sales promo-*			
	Number of accounts	*Total $ (000's)*	*Ave. per A/c. (000's)*	*Total $ (000's)*	*Ave. per A/c. (000's)*	*Ave. per 100 $ turn-*	*Total $ (000's)*	*Ave. per A/c. (000's)*	*Ave. per 100 $ turn-over*
Category A Ltd service retailers	10	1250	125	140	14	11	120	12	9.6
Category B Full service retailers	250	2800	11	916	4	33	250	1	9
Category C Wholesalers	15	3000	200	480	32	16	170	11	6
Category D Distributors	20	4450	223	615	31	14	170	7	2
Category E Direct to end-users	30	1250	41	240	8	19	90	3	7
TOTALS	325	12 750	39	2 391	7	19	800	2	6

value added). As a further quantification we have also included the physical number of distribution points and the sales volumes. The calculation of this quantification is also shown because of its importance. We have found that it is often wise to explain the calculations, and attach them to the distribution table because you may find that management does not like the results and therefore tends to question the figures. One further step you can take in order to make the understanding complete is to allocate the 'costs' to the specific distribution channel category (Table 8.4).

However it is worth saying that this is often very difficult as the records of most companies are not kept in a manner which is conducive to this calculation. If distribution is a critical element of the overal marketing mix, then even if you have to use some form of allocation resulting from your discussions with field sales management, it is worthwhile.

In the case we have detailed here, we can see some disturbing factors. The real resources which distribution costs the company are very high—forty-six per cent of total value added, and at $4 123 000 a high real monetary value. This may well be justified because of the nature of their business, but when one begins to look at the resources allocated to the specific channel categories and the return the company

Logistics			Total costs			Ave.	Gross profit		
Total $ (000's)	*Ave. per A/c. (000's)*	*Ave. per 100 $ turnover*	*Total $ (000's)*	*Ave. per A/c. $turnover*	*Ave. per 100 from list*	*Ave. discount (000's) price*	*Total $ (000's)*	*Ave. per A/c. turnover*	*Ave. per 100$*
52	5	4	312	31	25	40%	537	53	43
530	2	20	1696	7	44	33⅓%	1402	6	50
150	10	5	800	53	23	48%	1200	80	40
150	7	3	935	45	16	44%	1824	91	41
50	2	4	380	13	30	40%	537	18	43
932	3	7	4123	13	32		5500	17	43

obtains, then some obvious questions need to be raised.

From the cost and revenue analysis we can assess the 'profitability' of each category (see Table 8.5).

We see that Category B is totally unprofitable. With so many accounts to cover, the costs are extremely high, so despite the high gross profit the end result is a loss. Our total service provided is too high and we therefore need to look for a different approach. Perhaps handling the larger volume accounts ourselves and switching the remainder to being supplied by the wholesaler would be a potential solution.

Table 8.5. Analysis of profitability by category

000's omitted

	Category				
	A	*B*	*C*	*D*	*E*
Sales	1250	2800	3000	4450	1250
Gross profit	537	1402	1200	1824	537
Costs	312	1596	800	935	380
Profits	225	(194)	400	889	157
Profits as a % of sales	18%	(7%)	13%	20%	12%

Table 8.4. Specific allocation of distribution costs

Profit contribution statement		*Value added*			*Resource requirement of distribution*		
Sales	$12 750		$			$	Value added
Total cost of sales	7250	Manufacturing	3800	43%	Field selling	1400	16
Gross profit	5500	G & A	600	7%			
Sales Commissions	628	Field selling	1400	16%	Commissions	628	7
Freight	632	Commissions	628	7%	Royalties	121	1
Royalties	121	Royalties	121	1%	Sales office	250	3
Total variable	1381	Adv + sales prom.	800	9%	Total sales service	2391	27%
Field selling	1400	Marketing	250	3%			
Advertising & sales prom.	800	Sales office	250	3%	Advert. + sales prom.	800	9%
Marketing	100						
Total semi variable	2300	Shipping & freight	932	10%	Shipping & freight	932	10%
Contribution	1819	Total marketing	8781	50%	Total logistics	932	10%

Allocation of fixed/general overhead:		Other	100	1%		*Total turnover*	*Distribution points*	*Average per account*
Marketing	150				Category A	1250	10	125
Shipping	300				Category B	2800	250	11
G & A	600	Total value added	8881	100%	Category C	3000	15	200
Sales office	250				Category D	4450	20	223
Financial charges	100				Category E	1250	30	41
Total fixed	1400							
Pre-tax profit	419				Total	12 750	325	39

n.b. = 000's are omitted

n.b. = rounding off % figures accounts for line items adding up to more than 100%

Whatever the final solutions, this type of analysis gives you a very good perspective of the total situation—the services provided, the cost of those services and the contribution to overall profits that each category represents. The objective is to understand fully distribution as a whole because of the general high percentage of total company costs it represents. Within this cost structure often lies the key to greater profitability. A five per cent cost saving here will contribute far more towards increased profits than saving twenty per cent on the advertising budget.

Distribution channel suitability

The next step in the distribution audit is to evaluate the channel being used against the marketing needs of the company. Normally this is a purely quantitative assessment, but is nevertheless important. We are looking for the best channel fit to our target markets and in doing so:

Evaluating channel objectives and constraints.
Evaluating channel alternatives.
Selecting channel combinations.

Often the key to this evaluation lies in establishing and understanding the target customers. It still surprises us when we find a company using certain distribution channels because traditionally they always used them, regardless of the fact that their target groups, and in many cases their products, have changed dramatically over the years. It is therefore essential that before you start your audit process you have a clear and precise understanding of the priority target groups of the company. If they do not exist, the channels being used will only be the right ones by accident.

Determining channel objectives

The objectives will be determined by a number of factors and you must, as far as is possible, obtain answers to the questions being raised. The objectives will depend on:

Target audience analysis

Number of potential customers.
Geographic location.
Urban/rural.
Purchase habits including frequency and quantity bought.
Attitudes towards different sales and promotion techniques.

Product requirements

Unit value.
Durability (perishability).
Service requirements, before or after sale.
Product range.
Storage and handling requirements.
Display requirements.

Competitive situation

Channels they use.
Their strength in the channels.
Strength and weakness of products.
Market share.

Company capability

Size and financial strength.
Location.
Image.
Marketing strength.

Environmental conditions

Legislation.
Overall economic conditions.

Channel availability and conditions

Total number and locations.

Classification.
Degree of influence with target audiences.
Terms and conditions of sale requirements.
Storage facilities.
Sales effectiveness.

Answers to these points will determine:

Whether the company really knows what it expects from the distribution channels.
Whether the channels meet the company requirements.
What the limiting factors are.

Determining the channel alternatives will normally become clear, if the answers to the above points are known. The alternatives will also reflect the company's desires for:

Distribution intensity (exclusive, mass, selective, etc.).
The task it expects distribution to perform.
Degree of service the company is prepared to offer.

At this stage in the analysis we must determine that the channels being used are the most suitable and effective, our judgement being based on the quantitative answers and information we have obtained—the quantitative or economic evaluation being completed in the early part of the chapter. This quantitative judgment should consider:

Channel motivation capability.
Channel loyalty to company, brand, product range.
Conflict between various channels being used.
Adaptability of channel to changing market trends.
Changing trends within the channels.

Finally the effective use of channels and the overall channel strategy needs to be evaluated carefully by assessing its suitability and effectiveness to react or cope with the changing marketing requirements of the company. The company that makes basic changes to its marketing strategy, for example a decision to market private label products, without due consideration to its total distribution channel approach is not an unusual occurrence. The type of criteria we are looking for would include:

How the company adapts its channel strategy to cope with:

Emergence of new classifications of outlets.
Changing patterns of retail sales.
Changing customer purchase habits.
New or increased competitive pressure.
Lack of penetration of outlets.
Private label development.
New customer target groups for existing products.
Changing customer service requirements.

Channel audits

Adding or dropping channels through economic analysis.
Impact on competition or adding/deleting channels.
Effect on other channels.

Distribution channel classification analysis

As we said earlier, it is normal for companies to utilise a fairly wide variety of channels for their products. Yet often the detailed knowledge of the importance of each classification is not analysed. We always know our top five accounts but it gets hazy when we start to dig deeper. So to complete the quantification part of the distribution audit we now look at both the classifications being used and their relative importance to the company.

Whatever the combination of channels being used, they can always be 'classified'. Often this classification is a known and published listing within a country. Government departments, industry associations, even retail associations will have classifications lists. Where possible we find it desirable to use these prepared listings, if for no other reason than it gives you basic statistical information which you can use to measure your own performance against. The basis of the classification is usually one, or a combination, of the following:

Product category: photographic; hardware; food; electrical appliances etc.

Ownership: independent; group.

Location: urban; rural.

Type of channel: retail; wholesale; distributor; chain; multiple group.

Whatever the classification being used it is important to understand the relative quantification of each sector. One such analysis is detailed in Table 8.6. The table is fairly classical in its approach, with the possible exception of the profit numbers. As marketing is all about profit it continually seems strange that most companies evaluate and quantify distribution in terms of sales only. With gross profit often varying according to channel type, and costs being different, the sales only quantification seems totally insufficient for any auditing purpose.

The tables provide us with the detailed information required and because they also show previous years' figures we can also get a feel of the trends. In the case shown we clearly see the importance of the regional wholesalers and the trend of their increased share of the total business. Because of their small numbers they are critical to the business and we must therefore ensure that the right resources are allocated to ensure we do not lose them. Our marketing strategies can be reviewed with this in mind and actions taken if, for example, we see most of the resources being allocated to supporting the independent retailers.

Important customers

Following the classification analysis we now look at the most important customers. This refines even further our knowledge

Table 8.6. Distribution channel analysis Artists Oil Company

Classification	*Code No.*	*Prior Year*				*This Year*			
		No. of A/C's	*Sales volume*	*Gross profit*	*% of company sales*	*No. of A/C's*	*Sales volume*	*Gross profit*	*% of company sales*
General wholesalers	01	2	120	47	1	1	100	40	–
Office supplies wholesalers	02	8	1480	577	12	7	1500	600	12%
Stationery wholes.	03	6	1200	468	10	8	1400	560	11%
Stationery dealers	04	150	2000	960	16	160	2100	1005	16%
Stationery chains	05	12	450	216	4	10	400	191	3%
Mass merchandisers	06	15	450	216	4	15	500	239	4%
Dept. stores	07	80	1000	480	8	75	1050	504	8%
Office supplies distributors	08	10	1000	410	8	10	950	390	7%
Office equip. distr.	09	4	1400	574	12	4	1500	615	12%
School suppliers	10	4	1500	615	12	4	1400	574	11%
Laboratory supp.	11	1	600	246	5	2	600	245	5%
Government–direct	12	4	200	86	2	6	250	107	2%
Commercial–direct	13	10	450	193	4	12	500	214	4%
Industry–direct	14	6	300	129	3	8	300	129	2%
Misc. – direct	15	4	150	64	1	4	200	87	1%
TOTAL		316	12 300	5281	100%	325	12 750	5500	100%

of who is really important to our business—where both our strengths and potential weaknesses are. The eighty/twenty rule often applies, but it is amazing how many managers do not take practical note of it. When the eighty/twenty rule does apply most companies appear to react in one of two ways:

They ignore it and end up with crisis meetings when one or two of the top ten accounts have gone to competition.
They bend so much to important customers that the customers determine the company's actions with the management wondering why their profits are falling.

Somewhere in between is the right compromise, with the compromise being a predetermined strategy and not a strategy by default.

From Table 8.7 we can see the importance of our top accounts to the total business. We see that whilst the percentage of total sales has fallen from forty-four to forty-one per cent, their contribution to overall gross profits only fell by one per cent. We also see that two accounts have disappeared completely from the top ten listing, obviously requiring an explanation. The questions can go on and on, all of them giving you that extra insight into the total distribution picture. The only quantification that now remains is to look at the total number of accounts and relate them to the total turnover (Table 8.8).

Table 8.8. Accounts related to turnover

Accounts		*Sales volume*		*Gross profit*		*Gross profit*
% of total	*Actual number*	*% of total*	*Value*	*% of total*	*Value*	*%*
5%	16	49%	6230	45%	2500	40%
10%	32	61%	7800	59%	3245	42%
50%	162	85%	10 900	83%	4565	42%
75%	244	90%	11 500	89%	4895	42.5%
100%	325	100%	12 750	100%	5500	43%

Table 8.7. Top account analysis

(000's omitted)

Ranking *1976*	*1977*	*Customer's name*	*Cat.*	*Code*	*Sales value* *1976*	*1977*	*% of company sales* *1976*	*1977*	*Gross profit* *1976*	*1977*	*% of company G.P.* *1976*	*1977*
2	1		C	02	900	950	7.8	7.5	365	370	6	7
1	2		D	08	950	850	8.3	6.7	400	350	7	6
3	3		C	02	700	800	6.1	6.3	280	318	5	6
4	4		C	03	600	540	5.2	4.2	246	221	4	4
–	5		D	08	200	480	1.7	3.8	86	200	-	4
5	6		D	10	400	450	3.5	3.5	172	193	3	3
7	7		D	09	380	320	3.3	2.5	164	138	3	2
–	8		C	03	200	300	1.7	2.4	82	123	-	2
5	9		D	11	400	290	3.5	2.3	172	125	3	2
8	10		A	05	350	250	3.0	2.0	161	115	3	2
					5080	5230	44.0	41.0	2128	2153	40	39

NB The category refers to distribution category A, B, C, etc. mentioned on pp 177–8. The code is the channel classification code number from Table 8.6.

We have now collated all the information we required. It should be noted that whilst we have concentrated on looking at channels of distribution, similar techniques can also be applied to direct distribution, the ultimate customers taking the place of distribution classifications, value percentages to the total business and so on.

Sales force

In auditing the sales force function it should be made clear that we are not conducting a full scale evaluation of the sales force from a sales management viewpoint. That is a subject which is almost a book in itself. We are looking at the sales force from a marketing viewpoint, which means that many aspects of effectiveness of the sales force are not covered here. The quality of the sales presentations, record systems, training, sales aids, etc. are not dealt with. One may get involved in those matters should the overall sales force audit indicate that it leaves a lot to be desired. With sales forces varying so much from industry to industry and country to country, an effective evaluation tends to be very specific to the company being looked at.

There are however some very critical points which the marketing management can and should evaluate. But beware, sales managers are often the most ferocious of all managers; many seem to believe that only a sales manager should attempt an evaluation of the sales force, because how could anyone but a sales manamer really understand that part of the universe known as the 'field'? Their attitude towards change is almost Victorian and 'marketing is ninety per cent sales anyway'.

So what are we, as marketing men, looking for in auditing the sales force? Well first, salesmen cost money—not just in terms of salary cost, but also in terms of expenditures to put them out in the 'field' and the materials and support needed to do their job. In return, they bring in revenue in the form of sales volume and hopefully management manages this revenue down to a profit.

Our first evaluation point is therefore their cost and revenue performance (see Table 8.9).

Table 8.9. Salesmen cost/revenue matrix

000's omitted

Salesmen and territory no.	*Sales volume*	*% of target*	*Gross profit*	*Total cost*	*Cost per 100 units of sales value*
150	160	105%	67	35	21.8
151	210	80%	100	46	21.9
152	130	85%	65	40	30.1
153	250	95%	102	42	16.8
154	105	110%	58	38	36.2
Total	855	93%	392	201	23.5

In analysing a cost—revenue matrix a number of points must be considered:

How valid is the target?
How does the target relate to the potential of the territory?
What customer mix is contributing to the variable percentage gross profit situation?
What is the historical target by territory and performance against this target?
Allocate the sales management cost to the territory cost based on the total number of salesmen not the sales value of the territory.
Cost per hundred units of sales volume is critical because it is the direct cost of the sales revenue from the territory.

The matrix can be taken one step further by looking in more detail at the costs and the gross profit (Table 8.10).

From this analysis we see that not only does territory 154 'contribute' the least amount of direct contribution to profits, it also costs the most per unit of gross profit generated.

Obviously, we have shown quite simple examples; in a real

Table 8.10. Costs of sales force and gross profit

000's omitted

Territory No.	*Total cost*	*Total gross profit*	*Cost per 100 units of gross profit*	*Direct contribution*
150	35	67	52	32
151	46	100	46	54
152	40	65	61	25
153	42	102	41	60
154	38	58	65	20
	201	392	51	191

business the variances will be much greater and often obvious. Another rule of thumb step we often take in auditing salesmen's profitability is to take the profit they 'contribute' from Table 8.10 and try to take it down to a pre-tax or total profit contribution figure. Whatever financial information and reports are available, it is fairly simple.

From the statements all costs can be expressed as a percentage to sales—general and administrative, advertising, marketing, research, financial charges, customer service, etc. These percentages are then applied to the territory sales as follows:

Let's assume the expenditure breakdown of the company can be summarised by these ratios to net sales:

General and administrative	4%
Advertising	8%
Marketing (without sales costs)	3%
Shipping, freight	5%
Financial charges	1%
Sales office	3%
Total	24%

We can now produce a 'mini' profit and loss statement by territory (Table 8.11).

Table 8.11. Profit and loss statement by territory

	150	*151*	*152*	*153*	*154*
Sales	160	210	130	250	105
Gross profit	67	100	65	102	58
Salesmen cost and % share of sales management	35	46	40	42	38
Profit contribution	32	54	25	60	20
Cost allocation (24% to sales)	38	50	31	60	25
Profits	(6)	4	(6)	–	(5)

We now see that only one territory is 'profitable' with another one at breakeven; the rest lose money. Now all the accountants and sales managers are screaming that you cannot look at it this way. Our little calculation may not be one hundred per cent accurate, but it does give us a clearer picture of the true worth of this particular sales group and its territories: overall it 'loses' $13 000.

Now to conclude this piece of analysis we have to answer the question 'How do we make the group profitable?' The sales approach will generally be to try harder, in other words to get closer to target in the territories under target. In most cases this means lower percentage gross profit because reducing price and increasing discounts, tend to be the ways to gain more sales volume; because it generates a lesser amount of gross profit, it means we need more sales— and more price reductions. Whilst not advocating that the 'try harder' approach should never be used, it should be chosen when evaluated against other alternatives. In this particular case, a realignment of territories and reducing the sales force by one person may be a much better way to make the total group profitable.

For this exercise we need to know the elements of the expenditure which are fixed. The following is a practical guide:

General and administrative	— normally fixed
Advertising	— let us assume fixed
Shipping and freight	— variable on sales
Financial charges	— fixed
Marketing (without sales cost)	— fixed
Sales office	— fixed

From the example we have used we can see that the costs, in real money, will be:

Fixed	$
General and administrative	34 000
Advertising	68 000
Financial charges	8 600
Marketing	25 000
Sales office	25 000
Variable	
Shipping — currently 5% on sales of $855 000	

If we now delete one territory—let us assume territory 152—then the sales will be reduced:

Total	855 000
Less territory 152	130 000
	725 000
Total gross profit	392 000
Less territory 152	65 000
	327 000

Our total sales force cost will be reduced by $40 000 to $161 000. This figure does not however include the allocation of the percentage share of the sales manager, so we need to add this cost (say $10 000) back to the figure to give us a total sales cost of $171 000.

We can now complete another 'rough' profit statement:

	000's omitted
Sales	725
Cross profit	327
Sales cost	171
Fixed expenses	160
Freight (5% of sales)	36
Total Expenditure	196
Profit	(25)

However, in real life, we would not lose the total sales volume because we removed salesmen. We can therefore easily compute the turnover needed to get to a profitable situation.

Additional sales volume	50	75	100
Gross profit (50% from territory 152)	25	37	50
Freight – 5% of sales	2.5	3.75	5
Profit	22.5	33.25	45

At $52 600 we break even and after that is a healthy profit. The judgement is therefore whether one third of the sales from territory 152 can be obtained by allocating customers to other territories. In most cases we find that reorganising the work and coverage is a more predictable move towards profitability than the 'try harder' alternative.

We said earlier that the sales force is really part of the whole distribution strategy of the company, so let us now look at its performance as it directly relates to distribution coverage. Many years ago, as practising sales managers, we used to analyse our salesmen's performances, based on calls per day, orders to call ratio etc. (See the example given in Table 8.12.) We still believe this to be the most practical and efficient method to use. We have developed it a little to include cost and gross profit, but it is still the basic system which we practised twenty years ago.

The analysis gives us good information on the salesmen's

Table 8.12. Salesmen's call analysis

	150	*151*	*152*	*153*	*154*
Total calls	212	190	175	220	200
Average calls per day	10.6	9.5	8.75	11	10
Total order value	16 000	21 000	13 000	25 000	10 500
Total no. of orders	90	85	94	110	105
Order to call ratio	2.3:1	2.2:1	1.86:1	2:1	1.9:1
Average order value	177	247	138	227	100
Average order value per call	75	110	74	113	52
Average gross profit per order	73	117	69	90	55

qualities in terms of closing orders, calls per day and order size. Before judging the pure numbers you need to make sure you understand all the circumstances of the territory; for example:

Urban/rural.
Service calls.
Account size.
Territory potential.

If one wants to get really sophisticated then similar statistical analysis can be completed detailing sales, calls, orders and so on against specific products or distribution channels. They can be used when necessary and naturally give a further insight into the performance and area strength and weakness.

One of the more difficult decisions one normally has to face is which territories to devote additional marketing resources to, not just in terms of supporting weak areas but also where the potential additional volume is. As the source of much competitive information is the salesmen, a useful matrix is one

Table 8.13. Market share and distribution share by territory

Area territory	*Market size units (000's)*	*Market share*	*Total competitive volume (000's)*	*Existing no. of accounts*	*Number of potential accounts*
150	1900	52%	902	140	120
151	2800	40%	1680	110	120
152	1400	60%	560	105	60
153	2500	42%	1450	140	100
154	1200	70%	360	120	50
Total	9800	49%	4952	615	450

which looks at the market share and distribution share by territory (Table 8.13).

Using this type of matrix enables you to see much more clearly the areas where additional resources could be applied, with good potential for a positive return. Territory 154 would clearly be not the place to invest for expansion.

The combinations of matrix that can be applied to the sales are endless—in fact one has to be careful not to get carried away with them. Our audit is often simple and straightforward, yet we complicate it by looking at situations from every conceivable angle, with the majority of them adding little to our knowledge. We are basically looking for:

The effective use and allocation of the sales force and its costs in contributing maximum profits.
The reduction of sales force costs and perhaps sales volume in order to improve profits.
An increase in costs and obviously sales volume to improve profits.

The sales force remains a valuable marketing tool and that it what it should always be—a marketing tool. It is not an entity in its own right—the sole generator of revenue for the company. We still love the sales manager who, when above forecast, walks round the office like Napoleon, his hand on his inside pocket full of orders; when below forecast, his finger wagging at those stupid marketing people who made the packaging too big/small/dull/bright . . .

Key audit points

1. Distribution often represents the single largest expenditure item the company has—and also the biggest opportunity to improve profits, so devote the right amount of time to the audit.
2. Do not believe what the 'office' people tell you—go out into the field and look for yourself.
3. If you are in a strange industry or country make sure you understand the terminology. For instance, 'dealer' means different things to different people.
4. Make sure you know what the distribution channel objectives and constraints are.
5. Are the company's distribution objectives clear, and understood by management?
6. Because the same channels have always been used, it does not mean they are the right channels.
7. Make sure you get the real information on the services provided to distribution. Real life is often a lot different from the product manager's office.
8. Always check discounts, terms and conditions of sale, freight etc. with other companies within the industry.
9. Classifying distribution by type of service provided is often much more illuminating than the traditional methods of classification.
10. Analyse all distribution costs in as fine detail as is possible.
11. Check you have the right distribution in the right geographic area.
12. Make sure your priority target groups use the channels you supply. The use of down-market channels to supply up-market customers happens all too often.
13. Make sure your product configurations, packaging, units, etc. fit the needs of distribution.
14. Find out the true reasons why competition gets shelf space.

15. Watch carefully for trend changes in distribution—they happen faster than you think.
16. Do not be shy of dropping channels—or adding them. If the facts support the decision — do it.
17. Make sure the most important distribution customers are known (or important users if you deliver direct). Monitor and analyse their performance.
18. Distribution is used by the company to make profits, not sales.
19. The sales force naturally looks at its performance in terms of sales—you must look at it in terms of profit.
20. Make sure the sales force objectives tie into the marketing objectives.
21. The salesman who consistently exceeds his target by untold percentages has the worst target.
22. Look for sales against territory potential, not target.
23. Look for sales targets which include product mix.
24. If you are trying to increase the salesman's calls per day, make sure his average order value, or order-to-call ratio does not suffer—or you will stand still.
25. Like advertising managers, salesmen always tell you how good it is going to be—or how bad.
26. Remember Murphy's Fourth Law:

'If in any problem you find yourself doing an immense amount of work, the answer can be obtained by simple inspection.'

9 Conclusion

'The successful people are the ones who can think up things for the rest of the world to keep busy at.'

D. Marquis

Now the survey is complete. All that remains is to draw the final conclusions, write a report, produce an action plan and establish controls to ensure the necessary changes are made as quickly as possible.

No company is perfect. In fact any marketing organisation which can survive such a thorough scrutiny without pages and pages of recommendations for change is a pretty good one.

Some of the final proposals could be rather unpalatable of course, recognising that we are dealing with people as a resource and also with the work and ideas of the marketing staff past and present. Nevertheless, we must still keep to our original objective of optimising profitability through the best possible use of marketing resources. If it hurts, so be it. We must only concern ourselves that the results and conclusions are factual, honest and as accurate as possible.

It is one thing to write a report. Quite another to ensure that it is implemented. The key to this lies in the way the document is handled once produced. Unless you, the auditor, have direct line authority over the marketing department, it would be totally wrong to present your report to them and expect them to follow it through. Without a doubt, this is the surest way of having many of your ideas surpressed and eventually forgotten. The only guaranteed way to make things happen is to present your report to the man at the top—divisional director, general manager, managing director or some other person at this level. Courtesy dictates, of course that the head of the marketing department should be invited to your presentation to answer questions, comment and disagree perhaps. But one must have acceptance at the top.

Given senior management acceptance, someone, usually the head of the marketing department, must be made accountable for ensuring that changes happen and to time. He must produce work programmes detailing events and timings. These two must be examined and accepted. All that is left, then, is to follow-up on his actions against the agreed timings. Elementary, you might think, but in most companies we have visited we have found reports gathering dust and forgotten which could well have improved these companies' fortunes. Unused because this last, simple stage was omitted.

But the best way of all to guarantee action is to quantify the incremental profits that will result. It is always possible to neglect recommended changes in practices and procedures but no one, not even the most conservative of senior managers, can ignore significant changes in his pre-tax profits.

Index